NOTICES AND DOCUMENTS

ILLUSTRATIVE OF

The Literary History

OF

GLASGOW

AMS PRESS
NEW YORK

*Drawn and Engraved by John Horsburgh,
from an original Medallion by Tassie, in the possession of
Mr Robert Foulis.*

NOTICES AND DOCUMENTS

ILLUSTRATIVE OF

The Literary History

OF

GLASGOW,

DURING THE GREATER PART OF LAST CENTURY.

William J. Duncan, Editor

PRINTED AT GLASGOW.
M.DCCC.XXXI.

Verbatim et literatim reprint, with appendix additional, limited to 350 copies.
Glasgow: Thomas D. Morison.
1886.

Library of Congress Cataloging in Publication Data

Duncan, William James, 1811-1885, ed.
  Notices and documents illustrative of the literary history of Glasgow during the greater part of the last century.

  Original ed. issued as no. 14 of the Publications of the Maitland Club.
  1. Printing--History--Glasgow. 2. Foulis, Robert, 1707-1776. 3. Foulis, Andrew, 1712-1775. 4. Art--Glasgow--History. I. Title. II. Series: Maitland Club, Glasgow. Publications, no. 14.
Z152.G4D83 1973   686.2'09414'35   75-164806
ISBN 0-404-52947-X

Reprinted from an original copy in the collections of the Columbia University Library. Page size reduced 10%.

Reprinted from the edition of 1831, Glasgow
First AMS edition published in 1973
Manufactured in the United States of America

AMS PRESS INC.
NEW YORK, N. Y.   10003

PRESENTED

TO

THE PRESIDENT AND MEMBERS

OF THE

𝔐aitland Club,

BY

RICHARD DUNCAN.

THE MAITLAND CLUB.

M.DCCC.XXXI.

THE RIGHT HONOURABLE

THE EARL OF GLASGOW,

[PRESIDENT.]

    H. R. H. THE DUKE OF SUSSEX.
    ROBERT ADAM, ESQ.
    ROBERT AIRD, ESQ.
5 JOHN BAIN, ESQ.
    JOSEPH BAIN, ESQ.
    ROBERT BELL, ESQ.
    THE MARQUIS OF BUTE.
    ALEXANDER CAMPBELL, ESQ.
10 LORD JOHN CAMPBELL.
    JOHN D. CARRICK, ESQ.
    HENRY COCKBURN, ESQ.

MAITLAND CLUB.

JAMES DENNISTOUN, ESQ.

JAMES DOBIE, ESQ.

25 RICHARD DUNCAN, ESQ. [TREASURER.]

JAMES DUNLOP, ESQ.

JAMES EWING, ESQ.

KIRKMAN FINLAY, ESQ.

REV. WILLIAM FLEMING, D.D.

20 WILLIAM M. FLEMING, ESQ.

JOHN FULLARTON, ESQ.

JAMES HILL, ESQ.

LAURENCE HILL, ESQ.

JOHN KERR, ESQ. [VICE-PRESIDENT.

25 R. A. KIDSTON, ESQ.

G. R. KINLOCH, ESQ.

JOHN GIBSON LOCKHART, ESQ.

JAMES MAIDMENT, ESQ.

THOMAS MAITLAND, ESQ.

30 J. H. MAXWELL, ESQ.

WILLIAM MEIKLEHAM, ESQ.

W. H. MILLER, ESQ.

WILLIAM MOTHERWELL, ESQ.

WILLIAM MURE, ESQ.

35 ALEXANDER M'DONALD, ESQ.

MAITLAND CLUB.

THE VERY REV. PRINCIPAL MACFARLAN, D.D.
WILLIAM MACDOWAL, ESQ.
ANDREW M'GEORGE, ESQ.
JOHN W. MACKENZIE, ESQ.
40 ALEXANDER M'GRIGOR, ESQ.
GEORGE MACINTOSH, ESQ.
DONALD MACINTYRE, ESQ.
ALEXANDER M'NIELL, ESQ.
ALEXANDER OSWALD, ESQ.
45 EDWARD PIPER, ESQ.
JOHN M. PAGAN, M.D.
WILLIAM PATRICK, ESQ.
ROBERT PITCAIRN, ESQ.
J. C. PORTERFIELD, ESQ.
50 HAMILTON PYPER, ESQ.
P. A. RAMSAY, ESQ.
WILLIAM ROBERTSON, ESQ.
SIR WALTER SCOTT, BART.
JAMES SMITH, ESQ.
55 JOHN SMITH, ESQ.
JOHN SMITH, YGST. ESQ.
WILLIAM SMITH, ESQ.
GEORGE SMYTHE, ESQ.

MAITLAND CLUB.

MOSES STEVEN, ESQ.
60 DUNCAN STEWART, ESQ.
S. D. STIRLING, ESQ.
JOHN STRANG, ESQ.
THOMAS THOMSON, ESQ.
PATRICK FRASER TYTLER, ESQ.
65 ADAM URQUHART, ESQ.
SIR PATRICK WALKER, KNT.
WILSON D. WILSON, ESQ.
JOHN WYLIE, ESQ. [SECRETARY.]

PREFACE.

IN presenting the following Notices and Documents to the Members of the MAITLAND CLUB, some apology may be deemed necessary for the substitution of a work of recent origin for one of earlier date,—and for the title which has been adopted.

Hitherto no work has appeared which contains much information regarding the literature of Glasgow, and the Arts connected with it, during the last century. The materials for such a work are so much scattered, that the editor conceived that an attempt to collect them might not be unacceptable.

In regard to the title, he is conscious that it seems to promise more than the contents of this volume will strictly warrant. At the outset of the work, he merely proposed to combine a few notices relative to Printing and the Institution for the Fine Arts, established by Robert and Andrew Foulis. In collecting materials with this view, a few incidental pieces of information regarding the literary history of the city came in his way:—these he felt unwilling to suppress, as they seemed to possess some interest, and were not unconnected with his subject. A more comprehensive title thus became necessary, and while he is aware that his information is in many cases both meagre and imperfect, he feels that, unless he had something new or important to communicate, any notices of the eminent persons whose memoirs have been written by Stewart, Traill, Craig, and Robison, would have been superfluous.

Several short biographies of Robert and Andrew Foulis have been published, but they seem to have been almost wholly taken from one source,—Lemoine's History of Printing. The late Earl of Buchan, so early as 1795, addressed a letter to Mr John Nicholls, at that time editor of the Gentleman's Magazine, in which he recommends that a more complete memoir of "the Elzevirs of Scotland" should be prepared for one of Pinkerton's biographical works, then publishing. In this letter it is also mentioned that Professors Anderson and Wilson would supply the necessary materials. The Earl seems at length to have taken the task into his own hands, and to have extended his researches to the literary and typographical history of Glasgow generally. In this work, the proposed title of which was "Anecdotes of Printing and Academical Literature at Glasgow," his Lordship was assisted by the late Dr Robert Anderson, but unfortunately it was never completed,—a circumstance the more to be regretted, as a large proportion of the Foulis papers have since perished by fire. The results of their investigations are now in the possession of Miss Anderson, of Edinburgh, by whom they were politely communicated to the editor through the medium of Dr Irving of the Advocates' Library.

About the year 1811 Lord Buchan wrote to Professor Richardson of Glasgow, requesting his reminiscences of the Foulises. The letter written in reply (quoted under the name of "Richardson's Letter") contains much original and interesting information. For access to this document the editor has to acknowledge his obligations to W. R. Gibb, Esquire, into whose possession a copy, with Mr Richardson's interlined corrections, came by descent.

The Catalogue of Books has been drawn up principally from the works themselves, and with the assistance of Mr D. Macvean, who furnished a very large mass of materials for it, many of which, and especially the smaller pamphlets, might have been searched for in vain.

Unfortunately no document remains from which the completeness of the Catalogue can be proved, but it is probable that from the variety of the sources from which it has been compiled few articles of importance have been omitted. Those for which dates have not been found are added in a separate List, with a few which were ascertained after the first part of the Catalogue was printed. The sizes and original "trade prices" of the books in sheets are also affixed from a Catalogue of the Stock of Messieurs Foulis, for which the editor is indebted to the kindness of David Laing, Esquire, Secretary to the Bannatyne Club. To Mr Laing he has also to acknowledge his obligations for the Catalogue of Paintings,—which is the only remaining record of the works produced at the Glasgow Academy,—and for many other favours.

The editor has also offer his thanks to the Very Reverend Principal Macfarlan and to William Meikleham, Esquire, for the readiness with which access to the University and College Records has been afforded him,—to Dr Irving, for several interesting papers relative to Dr James Moor and to the Literary Society, printed among the Original Papers,—and to the Reverend Dr Fleming, Professor of Oriental Languages in this University, whose relation, Mr John Fleming, was the corrector of the Foulis press, and who has left some curious notices in his Diary, which unfortunately came too late to be embodied in the early part of the work.

As an illustration, an engraving from a medallion of Robert Foulis, by Tassie, has been prefixed. It is considered by one of his very few surviving friends an excellent likeness.

In conclusion, it may be necessary to state that the first part of the Notices of the History of Printing, extending from 1638 to about 1740, does not contain by any means a complete enumeration of the Glasgow printers. This has been recently given by Mr Macvean in his edition of M'Ure's History of Glasgow, and the repetition of it was therefore unnecessary. The editor's only object was, to introduce as much of it into this volume as would convey a correct idea of the state of the art, when Mr Foulis began to practice it.

W. J. D.

DECEMBER, 1831.

CONTENTS.

	PAGE
NOTICES regarding the History of Printing in Glasgow,	1
Catalogue of Books printed by Robert and Andrew Foulis,	49
Notices regarding the Academy established at Glasgow by Robert and Andrew Foulis,	81
Catalogue of Pictures, &c. done at the Academy in the University of Glasgow,	91

ORIGINAL PAPERS, containing,

I. Propofals for erecting a Bookfellers fhop and a printing prefs within the Univerfity of Glafgow, ... 119
II. Agreement between the Colledge of Glafgow and Donald Govane yōr, 120
III. State of the University at the beginning of the eighteenth century, 122
IV. Notice of Dr James Moor, ... 127
V. Notice of the Literary Society, ... 132
VI. Robert Foulis's last Letter to his Partners, ... 136
VII. Statement of Paper used by Robert and Andrew Foulis, from 1742 to 1765, 138

APPENDIX to New Edition, ... 145

NOTICES

REGARDING THE

HISTORY OF PRINTING

IN

GLASGOW.

NOTICES

REGARDING THE

HISTORY OF PRINTING

IN

GLASGOW.

THE Art of Printing was introduced into Glasgow by George Anderson in 1638,*—the same year in which the memorable General Assembly met there, and one of the first works printed by him was "The Proteſtation of the Generall Aſſemblie of the Church, and of the noblemen, barons, gentlemen, borrowes, miniſters, and commons; ſubſcribers of the Covenant, lately renewed, made in the high Kirk, and at the mercate Croſſe of Glasgow; the 28, and 29, of November 1638."† Anderson appears to have come to Glasgow in consequence of an invitation from the magistrates,—they agreeing that, besides an annual salary, he should receive a compensation for the expense of removing from Edinburgh. The following is the first notice of him on the records of the town council:—"4th January 1640. The ſaid day ordaines the theſaurer to pay to George Anderſon, printer, ane hundreth pundis, in ſatiſfaction to him of the ſuperplus he deburſit in tranſporting of his

---

* M'Ure's Hist. new edit. p. 368.

† Small 4to. eight leaves. It is also printed in The Large Declaration concerning the Tumults in Scotland, by Charles I., pp. 294—302.

gear to this brughe, by the ten dolloris he gave him of befoir to that effect: and als in fatiffaction to him of his haill bygane feallis fra Witfonday in anno 1638 to Martimes laft."* Anderson was succeeded by his son Andrew, who appears to have printed in Edinburgh in 1654-1655. He commenced printing in Glasgow some time afterwards, and continued there till about 1661, when he returned to Edinburgh.† Having obtained the appointments of printer to that city and college,‡ he in 1670 began printing an edition of the New Testament in black letter, but it was so disgracefully inaccurate that the Privy Council, on the 9th of February, 1671, ordained him "to receive from the ftationers all the copies remaining unfold," and prohibited him under a penalty of £100 sterling from reissuing it, until it should be revised and a new Title Page prefixed to it. Notwithstanding this transaction, which one would suppose would have ruined his character as a printer, Anderson was, within three months from that date, appointed his Majesty's sole printer for Scotland.‖

Anderson was succeeded in Glasgow by Robert Sanders, who styled himself Printer to the City, and who was for many years the only printer in the west of Scotland. But his unworthy predecessor, the royal typographer, being determined to enjoy his monopoly to its fullest extent, proceeded to Glasgow, and by threats or fair promises prevailed upon Sanders' workmen to desert him "in the midft of ane impreffion [of the New Testament] to his heavie loffe and prejudice." This op-

---

* Tabula Naufragii, No. 19.

† M'Ure, new edit. p. 368.

‡ On 10th June, 1663, "The Magiftrates appointed Andrew Anderfon to be ordinar printer to the good Town and College of the famen, in place of Gideon Lithgo, deceafed, during pleafure, he ferving als well and als eafie in the prices as utheris."—Chalmers' Life of Ruddiman, p. 100.

‖ Memorial for Bible Societies in Scotland, by Dr. John Lee, pp. 116–118.

pressive action brought the matter before the Privy Council, which decided, in December, 1671, that Sanders should be allowed to finish his book, and that every printer in Scotland had an equal right with his Majesty's to print the New Testament and Psalm Book in the letter commonly called English Roman. In 1680 the heir of Anderson complained to the Council that Sanders had vended Bibles printed in, and imported from, Holland, and that he had reprinted several works on divinity contrary to privilege. This charge having been proven against him by his own confession, he was ordained to deliver up the books so printed to the pursuer, but no other penalty was inflicted. He ultimately purchased a share of the royal patent, and having brought workmen and materials from Holland, printed several works in a creditable style.*

Sanders died, according to Watson, about 1696, leaving his printing establishment to his son, Robert Sanders, better known by the designation "of Auldhouse,"—a property purchased from a younger branch of the family of Maxwell of Polloc.† A few of the works first printed by him were tolerably executed, but his later productions are extremely paltry and inaccurate. Printing was now, and for some years afterwards, in the lowest state in Scotland. The exorbitancy of the royal grant to Anderson had produced the worst effects. No person appears to have been employed for the sole purpose of correcting the press, and the low wages given to pressmen, with the badness of the machines themselves, also tended to retard improvement.‡ To these may be added the following:—"There are two things hinder us in Scotland from printing,—pride and poverty. Pride,—in that we will print no-

---

* Lee's Memorial. App. p. 46—9. pp. 131—3. 120. Watson's Hist. of Printing, p. 13.
† Crawfurd's Renfrewsh., Robertson's edit. p. 35. M'Ure, new edit. pp. 368—9.
‡ Watson's Hist. of Printing, pp. 20—2.

thing that is common, whereas abroad the plaineſt and moſt common things are printed and reprinted every year, but we will not appear unleſs we have ſomewhat new and ſurpriſing to the world: And poverty,—we want money to print, and the people want it to buy books, and there is no ſale for them when printed." *

The University, in the meantime, was not wanting in efforts to improve the printing of Glasgow.† Mr George Ridpath thus writes to Principal Stirling in 1710:—" Mr Murthland wrote ſome time ago about a printer from hence. I ſpoke to one, but they want to know the particulars of their encouragem^t. 'Tis a bad time now for y^s preſſe is full of whats little worth, however, let me know your mind and I will do what I can." ‡

Probably this attempt was not successful, but the matter does not seem to have been overlooked. A paper, entitled " Propoſals for erecting a bookſeller's ſhop and a printing preſs within the Univerſity of Glaſgow," ∥ appears to have been presented to the Faculty in 1713, in which it is mentioned that they were " obliged to go to Ed^r. in order to gett one ſheet right printed." During the same year Thomas Harvie

---

* Wodrow's Life of Prof. Wodrow, pp. 170, 171.

† However inferior the execution, there seems to have been no lack of printers in Scotland at this period. "Sir," says John Anderson to his correspondent, "I know Edinburgh tolerably well. I did eat bread in it for the ſpace of twenty-five years: I know there are abundance of printing preſſes in it which want to be employed; and I, even when in a private capacity, never found any difficulty in getting a thouſand copies of a ſheet of paper thrown off in twenty-four hours; for when one would not, another would."—Anderson's Letters upon the Overtures concerning Kirk-Sessions and Presbyteries. Glas. 1720. pp. 5, 6.

‡ Letters to Princ. Stirling, MS. in Bibl. Univ. Glasg. This collection, which extends to four quarto volumes, was presented to Wodrow, the historian, by Stirling's widow, and formed part of the Wodrow collection of manuscripts.

∥ These " propoſals " are printed in Orig. Papers: No. 1.

a student of divinity, engaged to furnish " with all convenient difpatch, on or moe printing preffes, and at fartheft four years from the date hereof, to furnifh funts and other materials for printing Greek, Latin, & Hebrew; at leaft fo many of the laft Kind of Chara&ers, as are needfull to print a Grammar,"—under condition that he should be immediately declared University Printer and Bookseller for forty years, with " all the priviledges & Immunities which the Univerfity hath, or fhall have hereafter to beftow on their Printer & Bookfeller." Although these terms were probably not ultimately accepted, they seem at least to have been under frequent consideration, and the sketch of a contract with Harvie is preserved among the University papers. Two years afterwards, " Donald Govane, younger, merchant in Glafgow and printer," was appointed to the same office for seven years.* His name appears at very few books.

In 1718 the art of type making was introduced by "James Duncan letter founder in Glafgow." The types used by him are evidently of his own making,—rudely cut and badly proportioned. He deserves credit, however, for the attempt,—and his letters are little inferior to those used by the other Scottish printers of that period. He continued to print for many years,† and is well known as the typographer of M'Ure's History. In this book, which is not a creditable specimen of his work, he is styled " Printer to the City."

The precise date at which Robert Urie commenced printing is not known. Robert Urie and company were printers in the Gallowgate in 1740, and during the following year executed several works for Robert

---

* The contract between the College and Govan, which is curious, as showing what was required of a University Printer in these days, is inserted among Orig. Pap., No. II.

† M'Ure, new edit. p. 370. Duncan continued to print till about 1750.

Foulis.* They also printed the Glasgow Journal, which had been begun by Andrew Stalker in July, 1741.

The first newspaper published in Glasgow, appeared on the 14th of November, 1715, and was entitled "The Glafgow Courant. Containing the Occurrences both at Home and Abroad: Glafgow, Printed for R. T. and are to be fold at the Printing Houfe in the Colledge, and at the Poft Office."† It soon, however, changed its name, as the fourth number was published under the title of the "The Weft Country Intelligence." The following is a copy of the prospectus:—

"This Paper is to be Printed three Times every Week for the Ufe of the Countrey round, any Gentleman or Minifter or any other, who wants them, may have them at the Univerfities Printing Houfe, or at the Poft Office; its hoped this Paper will give fatiffaction to the Readers, and that they will encourage it by fending Subfcriptions for one Year, half Year, or Quarterly, to the above directed Places, where they fhall be ferved at a moft eafie Rate.‡

"Advertifements are to be taken in at either the Printing Houfe in the College, or Poft Office.

"The Gentlemen in the towns of Aberdeen, St. Andrews, Invernefs, Brechin, Dundee, St. Johnftoun, Stirling, Dumbarton, Inverary, Dumfries, Lanerk, Hamiltoun, Irwin, Air, Kilmarnock and Stranraer are defired to fend by Poft any News they have, and efpecially Sea-Port Towns to advife what Ships come in or fail off from thofe Parts."

---

* Ibid. p. 372. A few of these books will be found in the Catalogue of Works printed by R. & A. F.

† This curious article is preserved in the University Library.

‡ What this "moft eafie rate" was, is thus noticed in number 33. "N. B. This Paper is not fold in Retail under three half-pence, but for encouragement to fubfcribers, for one penny."

It is not known how long this paper was continued. The set of it in the College Library extends to the 1st of May, 1716,—being in all 67 numbers. It was printed on Tuesdays, Thursdays, and Saturdays, in a small quarto form (each paper containing twelve pages), and was made up of extracts from foreign journals, from the London newspapers, private letters, and occasional poetry,* with very little local intelligence.

The Glasgow Journal was begun under the editorship of Andrew Stalker, a bookseller, in July, 1741. With what degree of talent it was conducted for the first few years, it would be difficult to ascertain,—no copy of it during that period being known to remain. Fortunately the numbers from 1745 to 1749 have been recovered,—a period, one would suppose, sufficiently interesting. The editor, however, appears to have consulted his own personal security too much to permit him to give a firm and candid detail of the events which were then taking place. He has omitted several of the most important facts in the history of the Rebellion; and at length, when the danger approached his own door, was constrained to give vent to his terror in a letter which he inserted

---

* Let the following serve as a specimen :—

From the *Fling Post*.

M A R ALIAS R A M.

AN ANAGRAM.

Mar (read it Ram the other way)
Has made a Puſh, and loſt the day
And turns his Tail to Firth of *Tay.*
Perhaps (tho' ſo well taught to trick it)
Caught *by his back* in Highland Thicket,
At leaſt a Victim he may bleed
For leading wrong that ſhagged Breed,
Which now in doleful manner ſlain,
Cover the Fields about *Dumblain*, &c. &c. &c.

in the Journal. He had offended his readers by his omissions, and determined to retire for a time from his public duties. The following is his advertisement :—

"Oct. 14. [1745.] To the encouragers of the Glafgow Journal. Gentlemen,—I have carried on this paper fince the beginning, and, have, to the utmoft of my power, endeavoured to give an impartial account of facts as they happened; but finding that, confidering the fituation of affairs, *I cannot with safety publish so as to please the generality of my readers*, I have, therefore, given over being concerned in the writing or publifhing this paper till fuch time as the peace of this country be reftored, and have committed the care of it to an unexceptionable hand; and as you have favored me with your countenance and encouragement, I hope you'll continue to do fo to him; and am thankfully and refpectfully, Gentlemen, your moft humble Servant,

Andrew Stalker."

It would seem that this advertisement had been misunderstood, and to set the public right, Stalker published another letter in the next paper :—

"Oct. 21. To the encouragers of the Glafgow Journal.

"A wrong fenfe being put upon my laft advertifement, as if I intended entirely to drop this Paper, I hereby inform my Readers, that I continue to have the fame Share in it as formerly, tho' for fome time I am not to write it, nor collect the News from other Papers, Mr. Urie having undertaken that Part, who I'm convinced will give Satiffaction; and I hope that fuch as have hitherto been my Friends and Encouragers will continue to be fo.

Andrew Stalker."

Whether he resumed his editorship in quieter times, we are not informed: his name still continues as the publisher of the paper although immediately after the last letter appeared, Urie's name as printer was suppressed.

Yet whatever may have been the defects in the editorial department of this paper, it was printed in a style creditable in the highest degree to the town, and infinitely better than the newspapers published forty years afterwards.*

Urie continued to print very extensively in Glasgow till his death, which was occasioned by a paralytic attack on the 9th of February, 1771; † and although he was guilty of several piracies,—a practice in which he was probably encouraged by a decision of the Court of Session in favour of his friend Stalker in 1748,‡—yet he is undoubtedly entitled to the credit of restoring the respectability of the Glasgow press. Among the finest specimens of his work are his editions of the Greek New Testament and of the Spectator.

Robert Foulis, to whom we have already alluded, was the eldest son of Andrew Faulls,|| maltman in Glasgow, and of Marion Paterson. He was born in or near Glasgow on the 20th of April, 1707, and his

---

* The notices of marriages are somewhat amusing, as the following will show:—

March 24. 1746. On Monday last, James Dennistoun, junior, of Colgreine, Esq., was married to Miss Jenny Baird, *a beautiful young lady.*

May 4. 1747. On Monday last, Dr. Robert Hamilton, Professor of Anatomy and Botany in the University of Glasgow, was married to Miss Mally Baird, *a beautiful young lady* WITH A HANDSOME FORTUNE.

August 3. 1747. On Monday last, Mr. James Johnstone, merchant in this place, was married to Miss Peggy Newall, *an agreeable young lady,* WITH £4,000.

† Scots Mag.

‡ Falconer's Decisions, Vol. I. No. 256.

|| This was the original name of the family.

brother Andrew about five years afterwards.* During their earlier years, they were-educated under the care of their mother, who appears to have been a woman of plain good sense, and to have possessed a degree of knowledge considerably beyond her rank. She instilled into their youthful minds principles, which remained with them ever afterwards, and led them uniformly to speak of her with the greatest respect.

Robert was sent, probably at an early period, as an apprentice to a barber;—like his countryman, Allan Ramsay, he even seems to have practised the art for some time on his own account. It was while in this humble situation that the celebrated Dr. Francis Hutcheson, at that time professor of Moral Philosophy in the University, discovered in him that talent which was afterwards cultivated with so much success; he inflamed his desire for knowledge,—suggested to him the idea of becoming a bookseller and printer,—and although Foulis did not receive a complete University education as a preparatory step to this employment, he continued to attend for several years the lectures of his generous patron. Andrew, who seems to have been originally intended for the church, received a more regular education, and for some years taught the Greek, Latin, and French languages, and all the departments of philosophy then studied at the University. So ardently did the brothers pursue their private studies, that their lamp was seldom extinguished before midnight.†

The state of the University, in the earlier part of the eighteenth century, was sufficiently deplorable. When episcopacy was restored by Charles II., it had been deprived of a considerable part of its revenues,—

---

* Andrew was born 23d Nov. 1712. (Register of Births.) There were two younger brothers,—James, a clergyman, who died in America,—and John, originally a barber in Glasgow.

† Lord Buchan's Narrative. Richardson's Letter, pp. 16, 17.

those derived from the rentals of church lands. The greater number of the professors had also embarked in the unfortunate Darien expedition;* and the turbulence of the students, with the disturbed state of the country, added to their grievances. About the period at which the Foulises were students, it began to recover from the effects of these "Troubles." The professorships of humanity and ecclesiastical history were revived, and those of oriental languages, civil law, medicine, and botany were founded.† A visitation took place in 1727, and the commissioners drew up a statute and act regulating the University, the most important part of which seems to have been that the professors of philosophy who had hitherto carried their students through the three courses of logic, ethics, and natural philosophy, should in future confine themselves to one of these subjects.‡ The time was now come when it should no longer be considered beneath the dignity of a learned University to permit English to be spoken within its walls. Dr Hutcheson had introduced the practice of lecturing in English, and by this means not only obscurity of language was avoided, but the ancient and tiresome method of dictating rendered unnecessary. His colleagues slowly followed his example.

Of the occupation of the Foulises for several succeeding years, little or nothing is known. In 1738 they went to England, visiting in their route the University of Oxford,—from thence they repaired to the continent, and after an absence of some months returned to Glasgow in November of the same year. They again went abroad in 1739, and resided several months in France. In these tours they had oppor-

---

* List of Subscribers to Darien Expedition.

† Memorial for H. Glassford, Esq. of Dugaldston, &c. pp. 13—26.

‡ Extracts from this "statute," with a few other papers relative to the University, will be found among Original Papers, No. III.

tunities of meeting with persons of considerable literary and scientific attainments; through the chevalier Ramsay, they had access to the best public libraries,—and by these means they acquired an extent of information which their private studies could never have given them. During the same periods they applied themselves to the study of the more rare and valuable editions of the Greek and Roman classics; and as these were then much wanted in Britain,[*] they collected a considerable number, and on their return sold them in London at such prices as amply rewarded their industry. Having thus acquired a pretty accurate knowledge of books, Robert began business at Glasgow as a bookseller in 1741, and in the following year the first productions of his press appeared. While abroad, he had compared the letters used by the different printers, and having at length fixed upon those of Robert Stephens[†] as the most elegant, he employed Messrs Wilson & Baine to execute fonts upon these models. He had also attended a printing house in Glasgow for a short time, and had thus acquired a knowledge of the minuter parts of the art.

From this sketch of the history of printing in Glasgow, it will be evident that Robert Foulis began his career as a printer under very advantageous circumstances. He was assisted in the correction of his press by George Ross, then professor of humanity in the University, " an elegant Latin scholar, and a modest and most amiable man,"—and by James Moor,[‡] at that time a tutor about the college, and afterwards

---

[*] " Whereas the far greater part of the Books taught in our Schools and Colleges *are imported from foreign places into this country,*" &c. &c. &c. See appointment of Ruddiman and Davidson, as printers to the University of Edinburgh, inserted in Chalmers' Life of Ruddiman, p. 101.

[†] Which of the three Robert Stephens,—whether the father, son, or grandson (Dibdin's Decameron, vol. ii. pp. 82—95), my authority does not mention.

[‡] For the few notices of Moor which have been preserved, see Orig. Pap., No. IV.

professor of Greek. Dr Alexander Wilson, too, had just then improved the method of casting types, and established a manufactory at the village of Camlachie, in the immediate neighbourhood of Glasgow. With this excellent man the two Foulises ever afterwards continued on terms of intimate friendship.*

To these advantages must be added the appointment of the elder brother as printer to the University shortly afterwards. The following is an extract from the Records :—

31ft. March, 1743. Robert Foulis having this day given in a petition to the Univerfity meeting reprefenting that he had provided himfelf with fine Types both Greek and Latin, and defiring he may be made Univerfity Printer, The meeting having feen fpecimens of his printing and found it such as he deferves very well to be encouraged, Did chufe the faid Robert Foulis into the office of Univerfity Printer, and grant to him all the Privileges belonging thereto upon this condition viz : that he fhall not ufe the defignation of Univerfity printer without allowance from the Univerfity meeting in any Books excepting thofe of antient Authors.

Jo[N.] Orr, Rector.
Rob. Simson, Cl. Univ.

The University did not require, as in former times, that a copy of each book printed at their press should be given gratis to the library. From the Records it appears, that Foulis presented a catalogue of the works he had for sale, and that a committee was then appointed to examine and report " what books in that catalogue they thought fhould be *purchased* for the public library."

---

* A biographical account of Dr. Wilson, by his Son, will be found in the Transactions of the Royal Society of Edinburgh, vol. x. pp. 279—297. Honourable mention is made of him in Foulis's folio edition of Homer, Preface.

The first books printed by Robert Foulis were principally on religious subjects. In 1742, he published a pamphlet relative to the State of Religion in New England, and Whitefield's plan for establishing an Orphan House in Georgia. This subject, which occupied at that time much of the public attention, led him into a controversy with Whitefield, the result of which, however, has not been ascertained.* Next year produced "Demetrius Phalereus de Elocutione," which Dr. Harwood has marked "a good edition," and which was apparently the first Greek book printed in Glasgow, though George Anderson's printing house had been nearly a century before supplied with Greek and Hebrew types.† In 1744, appeared the celebrated edition of Horace, the proof sheets of which, it is well known, were hung up in the college, and a reward offered to any one who should discover an inaccuracy. It was printed under the care of George Ross, professor of humanity in the University, "a man ever to be remembered with respect and regret."‡ According to Dibdin, its claims to "immaculateness" rest upon no foundation, there being at least six typographical errors.‖ Three editions of the same author were printed at subsequent periods, none of which are of any comparative value. By the year 1746, Foulis had printed eighteen

---

* Foulis's pamphlet does not seem to have sold rapidly. At the distance of thirty-five years after its publication, there were still forty copies on hand.—*Catalogue of Foulis's Stock*, 1777.

† Lee's Memorial, p. 114., note. Harwood, p. 79.

‡ Kenrick to Dr Wodrow, April, 1808. Buchan MSS. "Price of the Fine Paper, neatly bound, 3 fh. Common Paper, in Sheep, 1s. 3d."—Glasgow Journal, 15th July, 1745.

‖ The following is the list :—

Page 131, *line* 119, qnod *pro* quod.　　　*Page* 35, *line* 1, Lib. I.　　*pro* Lib. II.
— 128, — 29, nʋtus — natus.　　　— 178, — 41, Non est est　— Non est.
— 129, — 38, Tnne — Tune.　　　— 191, — 1, Epitolarum　— Epistolarum.

different classics, besides Dr Hutcheson's class-books, in English and Latin; and Homer, with the Philippics of Demosthenes were advertised as in the press. The Homer appeared in the following year, both in a quarto and an octavo form: the first of these is a very beautiful book, and more correct than the other, which was printed after Dr Clark's edition.[*]

It was probably about this period—for the exact date cannot be ascertained—that the first society for the discussion of literary and philosophical subjects was instituted in Glasgow.[†] Of this society Robert Foulis was an original member. It met every Friday evening at half-past five o'clock, from the first Friday of November to the second Friday of May; and if, during that period, any member was absent for four successive nights, without a valid excuse in writing, his name was struck off the list. Each member, in the order of seniority, read an essay on subjects connected with science, literature, or the arts. After this, the president requested the members to state their sentiments, and the orator was then at liberty to reply. In the discussions which followed, the order of seniority was not observed. When each member had read an essay, they in the same order brought forward a question, which they were bound to explain and illustrate, upon which discussions of the same nature as those already mentioned followed.

---

[*] Harwood on the Classics, p. 3.

[†] The dates relative to the institution of the society differ. Mr Craig, in his Life of Professor Millar, makes it in 1752, while Professor Richardson (Life of Professor Arthur) mentions that Dr Hutcheson explained in the society the works of Arrian, &c. Now Dr. Hutcheson died of fever in 1747 (Life by Principal Leechman). One of the surviving members has stated, that the first entry on the Records was Remarks on Harris' Hermes, by Mr. Clow, professor of logic, which was first published in 1750. The volume, in which these transactions are recorded, has not been recovered.

At the meetings of this society, Dr Hutcheson is believed to have explained and illustrated the works of Arrian, Antoninus, and the other Greek philosophers. Adam Smith read those essays on Taste, Composition, and the History of Philosophy, which he had previously delivered while a lecturer on rhetoric in Edinburgh. Several of those read by Dr Reid were afterwards published.* Professor Arthur descanted on the Principles of Criticism, and the Pleasures of Imagination; and a few of these papers were published after his death in his "Discourses on Theological and Literary Subjects."† Dr Black communicated his discoveries in chemistry,—particularly on the subject of latent heat. And Dr Moor illustrated Grecian literature, and the influence of the Fine Arts upon Society.‡

The discourses read before the society by the elder Foulis were generally on the Fine Arts, although sometimes on Philosophical or even Theological subjects; and it is mentioned by Professor Richardson, that in an essay on Crimes and Punishments, he seems to have anticipated the sentiments of the celebrated Becarria on these subjects.||

When he delivered his opinions in the Literary Society, his manner was more reserved than upon other occasions. Never forgetting the humble station from which he had risen, he had nevertheless a consciousness of

---

* Besides these, an essay on the Utopian System, read before the society by Reid, was printed in the Glasgow Courier, and is to be found reprinted in Appendix, No. 2., to Arthur's Discourses.

† Richardson's Life of Arthur, p. 515. App. to Discourses.

‡ A volume of Moor's essays was printed by R. & A. Foulis in 1759, 12mo. For a list of its contents, see Orig. Pap., No. IV. He also read an essay on the End of Tragedy according to Aristotle, which was published in 1763, 12mo. It was afterwards reprinted by Andrew Foulis, printer to the University, 12mo. 1794.

|| Richardson's Letter, p. 22. For a list of the essays read by Robert and Andrew Foulis, see Orig. Pap., No. V. Andrew Foulis's discourses were on miscellaneous subjects.

moving precisely in his proper sphere, and of having deserved that distinction which he had attained.*

The success which had attended the efforts of the Foulises as printers, induced the elder brother to extend the sphere of his usefulness. The following extracts, from what appears to have been the first draft of a letter, contain a rapid sketch of his plans for fourteen years previous to the institution of the Academy. No apology will, therefore, be necessary for the style in which it is written. "In the years 1738 & 1739," says he, "having gone abroad, and refided for feveral months at each time at Paris, we had frequent opportunities of converfing with gentlemen of every liberal profeffion, and to obferve the conneƈtion and mutual influence of the Arts & Sciences upon one another & upon Society. We had opportunities of obferving the influence of invention in Drawing & Modelling on many manufaƈtures. And 'tis obvious that whatever nation has the lead in fafhion muft previoufly have invention in drawing diffuf'd, otherwife they can never rife above copying their neighbours. Tho' we were convinced of this early, and wifh'd to fee the manufaƈtures of our own country enjoying the like advantages, yet the attempt requiring more money than we were mafters of, we contented ourfelves with importing old editions of Greek and Latin Authors, which were very much wanted at that time in Scotland.—In the year 1743, I went to France alone partly to try the fortune of our firft effays in Greek and Latin Printing, partly to bring home fome Manufcripts, partly to colleƈt more ancient authors, and to have brought a fingle Graver, if a good one could have been had on reafonable terms. The Rebellion coming on foon after, prevented all fcheming for a time: Soon after it we found ourfelves engag'd in the printing of Cicero & fome other expenfive works, which occupied all our time, money &

---

* Richardson's Letter, pp. 6, 7.

credit. In the year 1751, I went abroad for the 4th time in company with a younger brother, and fpent near two years; the firft months were fpent in Holland in exchanging Books of our own Printing whether Greek, Latin or Englifh, and in enquiring after affiftances for adorning an Edition of Plato. Before this journey was undertaken, the fcheme of an Academy had been pretty well digefted, and often the fubject of debate in private converfation."*

Robert Foulis, having previously sent home his brother with a painter, an engraver, and a copper-plate printer, whom he had engaged in his service, returned to Scotland in 1753, and soon after instituted his Academy for painting, engraving, moulding, modelling, and drawing. The University allowed him the use of what is now the Faculty Hall as an exhibition room for his pictures, and of several other rooms for his students; and three Glasgow merchants, with a liberality which reflected the highest credit upon themselves, afterwards became partners in the undertaking. These were Mr Campbell of Clathic, Mr Glasford of Dougalston, and Mr Archibald Ingram,—the last a man certainly of no literary pretensions, nor even liberally educated, but possessed of intelligence and public spirit. The students, according to the proposed plan, after having given proofs of genius at home, were to be sent abroad at the expense of the Academy.

The whole scheme seems generally to have been considered as romantic, and we have Foulis's own testimony, that "there feemed to be a pretty general emulation who fhould run it moft down." This opposition, however, only increased his determination, and the Academy was continued long after he might have known that it would ultimately ruin him, if persevered in.†

---

* Incomplete Letter by R. Foulis, without date or address.—Ld. Buchan's MSS.

† For a farther account of the Academy, with the documents relating to it which have not been preserved, see Catalogue of Pictures, &c. reprinted in this volume.

Foulis often displayed a degree of firmness bordering, as in the present instance, on obstinacy. It will readily be believed that many of his friends attempted to dissuade him from his unpromising design,— among these was the Right Honourable Charles Townshend. In a conversation with the two brothers, that celebrated statesman (who entertained a great regard for them) took occasion to point out, in his usual forcible manner, the disadvantages under which they must labour, in establishing their Academy, and its almost certain ultimate failure. He addressed them with an eloquence so impressive, and exhibited such views of loss and disappointment, as converted Andrew to his opinion, and affected him even to the shedding of tears. On turning, however, to Robert, from whom he expected acquiescence, if no farther manifestation of his feelings, he found his resolution unabated.*

Nor was this the only dissuasive he received. His friend Mr. Harvock, secretary to the Earl of Northumberland, writes to him on the 20th of December, 1753, in the same strain :—

"My Lady [Northumberland] will be glad to fee your Prints when finifhed; but I cannot help thinking that my Lord is of my opinion, that a correct and well-printed Book would be more agreeable to us from your Prefs than any thing elfe. Thefe will ornament, and with great luftre too, as well as real profit, the Libraries of Popes and Princes, while your Prints lye mouldering in a Dufty Corner. Correct Printing, in an elegant form, is, I own, both laborious and expenfive, but then it has an intrinfic merit which ftamps a value upon it and the Printer to future ages; and the Book muft be efteemed as long as Reading is in fafhion. Elzevir was once in high efteem, and even fo late as my time. For what? for the beauty of his types,—but now our young men find

---

* Richardson's Letter, pp. 11, 12.

him ſo very incorrect that they uſe him chiefly both at Schools and Colleges in certain remote places where people may read a Page before they apply the leaf properly. I ſhall be very glad to ſee your Tacitus &c. when they come abroad. The Printing of the Dublin Edition is not quite to my mind. Ld. and Lady Northumberland will return from Bath in ten days, and then your Parcell will be opened. I really believe from what I have ſeen and heard, that not only the D. of Argyle, but all men of Senſe, wiſh you more ſucceſs in Printing than in Painting and Sculpture. We are overrun with Prints of all kinds; but good Printing will be deem'd a novelty ſince the days of R. Stephens, who minded only one thing; and pray conſider, he lay under more diſadvantages than you do now. Print for poſterity and proſper."

The following letter, containing an outline of the operations of the Glasgow press, was probably written in answer to that of Harvock soon after Foulis's return from the continent,—apparently about the beginning of 1754.

"I received and read juſt now your very obliging and kind letter. Among the firſt things I did after coming home was, to cauſe gather out and few them that I might be ſure they were complete. My intention was, to have ſent them off immediately but my Brother Andrew perſuaded me to delay until a new Edition of Mr. Hutcheſon's Elements of Moral Philoſophy was finiſhed, and an Edition of Roſcommon's Poems, the laſt of which is finiſhed this day and the Books go off with the Carrier to be Shipt, directed for my Lady Northumberland, at Northumberland Houſe, London: as to the reſt of my apology, it was vanity made me hearken to the voice of my Brother. I was ſenſible that all we have printed in Engliſh is too inconſiderable for the quantity, being chiefly a few ſmall Books in which we have aimed rather at neatneſs than ſplendor; and theſe not all books of entertainment. Such as they are, I have put them together, leaving you to reject what you think improper. However, I hope we shall with time print a variety in English more suitable to the favourable idea that her Ladyship is pleased to entertain of us. I own, I ought to have wrote to you in good manners, and I might have wrote a dozen letters with less trouble than I felt for neglecting that. Since I came down, I have been very busy going thro' a multiplicity of things that waited my arrival and I have been so negligent as to writing that I have scarce wrote to any friend in London since I left it. The Prefs is just now employed in printing Mr. Hutcheson's Large System of Moral Philosophy, for which my Lord Northumberland is already a Subscriber. I look upon this as a capital work for promoting the cause of virtue, accompanied with just notions of government and Liberty. Tacitus is above three-fourths advanced, from the quarto Gronovius Edition, in the same form, letter & paper with Cicero. The Aminta in Italian is just finished, in the same letter with our Lucretius. Plutarch's treatise on hearing the Greek Poets & Euripides' Orestes are likewise now come from the Prefs. We are also printing Shakespear according to Mr. Pope's Second Edition. The first volume was printed before I came down, and as the Plays are all printed so as to sell separately, we are going on with the rest not in order, but first with those which are most esteemed. I have not yet begun to print Plato, not only because I would have all prior obligations discharged, but because I would have as few things to repent in the execution as possible. I would have all helps amassed, and at least one Volume entirely ready for the Prefs before it be begun. I would be thoroughly satisfied with regard to the elegance of the Greek character which I use. I would have some researches for finding a better Ink than ordinary, fully made out in the meantime. I was informed last post that there is a large packet of collations from Plato from the Vatican. Mr. Moor, who thinks to have the first Volume ready for the Prefs in three months, is greatly pleased with yᵉ able Traguier's Commentary, which perhaps we will print entire. Our Lucretius is out of print or near by, fo that I fhall remember Comino's Gloffary on reprinting it. I will likewife take the firft opportunity of procuring Copies of his Plautus and Tully de Officiis, the one of which I have never printed, and the other I propofe to reprint foon. As the world had once too high an admiration of Ariftotle without underftanding or perhaps making the proper ufe of him, they have been for fome time fo much in the other extreme that few learned men have any general acquaintance with his works, fo as to know what they really contain. A few writers, like Mr Harris, might perhaps raife fuch a curiofity as might make him a little more *à la mode*. The prefent edition of Tacitus, which was half printed before I came here, is [in] a form that will not anfwer well with Notes, but if we fhould print it fome other time in a larger form and character."*

The edition of Plato, mentioned in this letter, had been projected as early as 1746, and it appears that proposals and a specimen of the work were printed about 1749,—soon after the large edition of Cicero's works was completed. In July, 1751, it has been already mentioned, Foulis went abroad,—carrying with him letters of recommendation from his brother-in-law, Dr Moor, to the Abbé Salier and the learned M. Capperonier, both of the Royal Library of Paris. He first spent some time in Holland, in the expectation of receiving assistance from Hemsterhuse and Alberti, and before returning to his native country had seen the best Manuscripts, and had given orders for collations from those in the Vatican and National Libraries. After his return, it would seem that the project was still under consideration, and that

---

* This sentence is left incomplete.

Dr. Moor, who from the multiplicity of his engagements had formerly declined taking charge of it, now undertook the editorship.* The design was not abandoned till 1759, by which time Foulis, in his enthusiastic love of the Arts, had extended his Academy far beyond the limits of prudence.

According to the plan proposed by Foulis, the Plays of Shakespeare were printed for several successive years in a separate form. " King Lear" was published in 1753,—" Richard III." in 1758,—" Coriolanus" in 1760 ; but it was not till six years after that they appeared complete. The small paper was in eight, and " a few copies printed on the fineſt foolſcap in Sixteen Volumes 8vo."

The following letter from Sir John Dalrymple, though evidently written in the style of a patron, contains some curious information, and is dictated by the warmest attentions to Foulis' interests. Lord Buchan marks it as " charaƈteriſtic."

SIR,—I have changed my mind about the Dedication to Mr. Hamilton's Poems. I would have it ſtand " the friend of William Hamilton," but I aſſent to your opinion to have ſomething more to expreſs Mr. Crawfurd's Charaƈter. I know none ſo able to do this as my friend Mr. Smith ; I beg it therefore earneſtly that he will write the Inſcription and with all the elegance & all the feelingneſs which he, above the reſt of mankind, is able to expreſs. This is a thing that touches me very nearly, and therefore I beg a particular anſwer as to what he ſays to it. The many happy and the many flattering hours which he has ſpent with Mr. Hamilton & Mr. Crawfurd makes me think that he will account his uſual indolence a crime upon this occaſion. I beg you will

---

* Dr Moor's Notes and Collations got into the hands of Mr. John Reekie, and were added to his copy of Ficinus' Plato. See Bibl. Reekiana, No. 39.

make my excufe for not wryting him this night about this. I confider wryting to you upon this head to be wryting to him.

Your things are come to Town. I am completely & perfectly pleafed with your Bufts. The Carrier let the large Antoninus fall juft at Yair's Shop Door, by which means the head was knocked off from the fhoulders; you will give Directions how to mend this, and in the mean time pleafe to make the Carrier pay the expence, becaufe without making an example thefe fellows will break your things every time they bring them in. I am much furprized you did not fend in the moft beautiful of all your things, the Faustina & young Antininos.* I was much difappointed in the picture in the Apollo teaching the young man to play on the Harp. It is by no means executed with Cochran's ufuall accuracy: the wrift of the young man is too fmall, his knee too large, his features juft bordering on the Grotefque, and the carnation of both the colour of the Earth. Your lads ought to copy the Pictures that they fee exactly, in the Dimenfions that they fee them, inftead of trufting to themfelves to make a little thing of a large one, or a large thing of a little one. The Holy Family of Widows Scholar † is beloved, and Cochran's Saint admired, but the things that will take moft, by which I mean that will fell beft, are Lawndfcapes. The moft ignorant can judge of the impropriety of a human figure or a human paffion, but it muft be only one accuftomed to look at the beautys of Nature, who can judge of a falfe ftep in a Lawndfcape. A Lawndfcape, too, hits the prefent tafte of ornamenting a room, by which I mean, making it more ugly than it naturally is; for which reafon I beg that you would employ your Boys in doing the beft of your Lawndfcapes becaufe I can make you certain that thefe

---

* This letter, which has been dictated to a blundering amanuensis, is grievously misspelt. The name should have been Antinous.

† Probably of Guido's scholar.

are the things that will fell beft. In the Hiftory-Pictures that you fend in, I beg you will take the advice of Mr Smith and Dr Black. Your prefent fcheme fhould be, to execute, not what you may think the beft, but what will fell the beft: In the firft, you may be a better judge, fince you are the Mafter of a great Academa, but in the laft I think their advice will be of ufe to you. Your Angel delivering St Paul is too large a Picture. Small things executed with care, will, I imagine, bring you moft in vogue: Such are The Holy Family, The Reading Saint, and The Three Angels Playing.

The Subfcription Paper, which I charged myfelf with, is now at Ninety Guineas. There are three more out, in the hands of Mr. Adam Ferguffon, Dr Cullen and James Adams. I have not yet got them in, but expect Twenty Guineas amongft the three. In the prefent view I have of the thing, I think I can carry my own Paper Twenty Guineas further, befides which I have a chance of Twenty Guineas more, for having by accident apportered * of a very worthlefs Anceftor of a very good Lady who has folicited me for it. I have confented to make her a prefent of it, provided fhe will bring Twenty Guineas of Subfcriptions to the common caufe, fo that by the end of the winter, I think I may infure you of a Hundred & fifty Gnineas, after which it is the fault of your Town and of your own Country, if they cannot fill up the remaining Fifty Guineas fo as to make the fubfcription Two hundred Guineas. I wifh you would get application made to Shawfield, for I have no communication with him. You need make no general application through your Town for ten days till I have got the Subfcriptions together, and then I fhall write a Circular Letter to many of your people with copies of the propofals & of the Subfcription.

If all this fhould fucceed to our wifhes, I fuppofe, my dear Robert,

---

* A Portrait?

D

you will think that the whole country of Scotland rifes in your caufe, but let me tell you, and let it make fome impreffion upon you, that you are greatly miftaken. With all the fine names that you fee at this Paper, I affure you that the motives of the Subfcribers need by no means encourage you. Some give their money, becaufe they are vain to do it; others becaufe they are afhamed not to do it : Many repented the moment they had done it. Some fubfcribe out of regard to me, and others merely becaufe they were teafed ; and of all this fubfcription which you fay, flatters you fo much, there are not five men who would give Ten Pounds to fave you from the Gallows or the Academa from the flames; for which reafon I do earneftly befeech you to retrench your Scheme and expence, inftead of extending it upon the hopes of the good will of your countrymen ; for take my word for it again, very few of them give one farthing either for the fine arts or for you, and for that reafon it is your duty in common fenfe to draw in your fcheme, to fell off all fuperfluities, and to bring it into a mercantile affair as much as you can. The Devil, without cloven feet and without a Tail is infinitely worfe than the Devil with both, and this truth you will find if you launch out into immoderate expence on the profpect of fuch a benevolence and fuch a love of Beauty as reigns in your own heart, and in exceeding few other places.

The Paris-Plaifter work feems to me a folid fcheme, if you contrive your prices fo as to underfell the London mercate here, and yet to make money to yourfelf. I once thought your cafting of Prints likewife a folid fcheme, becaufe they coft you little, and if you got half nothing for them you was ftill a gainer in cent per cent, but by some fatality or perhaps fome natural reafon which you may be able to account for, this has never come to any thing. I wifh you would difpatch your ftupid Boys, and keep only the choice Spirits among them fo as to leffen your expence. You are not to truft to this fubfcription, for in the firft place of this hundred & fifty guineas you will not draw above a hundred and thirty in, and befides it is a chance if one half of your Subfcribers do not withdraw next year; So again & again, my good friend, draw in your arms.

It is of confequence to you to be able to fupply the mercate at Edinburgh while the iron is yet hott; for that reafon I beg you will fend in one copy of every good Buft that you have to be Shown in Fleming & Yair's Shop, and befides that, with all the expedition you can that you will likewife fend in two more copies of each to be kept in Boxes in fome Wareroom till people make their choice of the different Bufts, for it is in thefe chiefly that I expect fale. I once thought it would have been beft for you to have allowed Commiffions to be fent to you to Glafgow, but I fee now that will not do, as people are impatient to have their things directly, & will take if delivered immediately what he [they] will not take if delivered eight days after this. Likewife fend a few more copies of your Pictures to be fold as any Body offers: Send Catalogues too of the Mafters, the Boy's name, the price, and likewife of the name of the Buft & the price. None of thefe things are done hitherto. Lord Selkirk talked to me of a project to get a Salary fetled upon you by the Government: he fpoke of this as if he had thought of it before hand, tho' like a man that did not care to fpeak of it unlefs he could fpeak of it with certainty. You will fee him at paffing & may talk to him. Further in the way, the Duke of Argyle fpeaks of you and with the fpirit of Mr Pitt's miniftry I fancy the thing may not be quite an Idea. Whether it is an Idea or not I am going to give you a piece of trouble: be fo good as make out a Catalogue of your Pictures, and as far as you can of your Bufts, Books of Drawings and Prints,—Secondly, of your Boys and how employed,—3dly, of the people who have ftudied under you with a view to the Mechanical Arts,—and laftly, Give fome account of the profpects which you think you have of being of ufe either to the Mechanical or the Fine Arts of your Country. Frame this into a Memorial and fend it to me; I fhall have it tryed here by some who wifh well to you, and as I go to London in the Spring I fhall, together with Mr. Wedderburn & Mr. Elliot, confider what are the moft prudent meafures to take for your fake, or whether to take any. Mr. Smith is too bufy or too indolent, but I flatter myfelf Dr. Black will be happy to make out this Memorial for you.

Let me know if I have any chance of feeing you this winter. I have none of being at Glafgow, and therefore wifh you & Mr. Smith would come here, or you by yourfelf would come here in the Christmas vacance.

I am, Sir, Your moft Humble Serv$^{t.}$

JOHN DALRYMPLE.

Edin$^{r.}$ 1 Dec. 1757.

The work referred to in the beginning of this letter was an edition of Hamilton of Bangour's Poems. They had first issued from the press of Robert and Andrew Foulis in 1749, without the name of the author, and avowedly without his knowledge or consent.

"No writings of this kind," says the editors, "ever had a better claim to the indulgence of the public than the following poems, as this collection is publifhed not only without the author's confent but without his knowledge, and therefore in juftice to him, the editors muft take upon themfelves any faults or imperfections that may be found in it.

"One inducement to print them," they continue, "was to draw from the author a more perfect edition when he returns to this country, and if our faulty attempt fhall be the occafion of producing a work that may be an honour to this part of the kingdom, we fhall glory in what we have done.

"What brought us at firft to think of this little undertaking was the concern fome of the author's friends expreffed to us at the edition of his noble poem of Contemplation lately publiſhed from an incorrect manuſcript: this determined us to give an edition of it leſs unworthy of the author and to join to it every piece of his that had been printed at different times, and we prevailed likewiſe on a friend of his, tho' with ſome difficulty, to give us a ſmall number of pieces that had never before been printed, ſome of which had been handed about in manuſcript and might have been printed with the tranſcribers errors by others. It is owing to the delicacy of this friend of the author's, that this edition is not enriched with many original poems and ſome beautiful tranſlations from Pindar & other ancient poets, both Greek and Roman, that are in his poſſeſſion, but which he would not permit to be publiſhed."

It is not wonderful that a second edition of poems which had been compared to those of Dryden or Pope should now be called for. It accordingly appeared with the author's name, and dedicated "to the memory of Mr. William Craufurd, Merchant in Glaſgow, the friend of Mr. Hamilton."*

These poems appear for some time to have attracted very little notice, and were, in fact, becoming almost forgotten, when the public attention was called to them by a criticism in the Lounger from the pen of Professor Richardson. In spite, however, of all their "regular deſign, juſt ſentiments, fanciful invention, pleaſing ſenſibility, elegant diction, and ſmooth verſification," they are now little read,—whether deservedly so, we shall not determine. Mr Richardson has given them their full amount of praise,—he shows (or attempts to show) that all the qualities above mentioned will be found in the poem of "Contemplation," while "the Braes of Yarrow" is pronounced to be "one of the fineſt ballads ever written." The opinion of Pinkerton on the same subject seems

---

* The edition published at Edinburgh in 1760, with the author's last corrections, and a profile of him by Strange, is the best edition of Hamilton's Works.

now to be generally considered the more correct. "It is," says he, "in very bad tafte and quite unlike the ancient Scottifh manner, being even inferior to the pooreft of the old Ballads with this title. His repeated words and lines caufing an eternal jingle, his confufed narration and affected pathos throw this piece among the rubbifh of Poetry."

To proceed in our account of the operations of the Glasgow press. The Select Society of Edinburgh had in the year 1755 determined to give premiums for improvements in the Arts, Sciences, Manufactures, and Agriculture. "The Art of Printing," say the Society, "in this country requires no encouragement; yet, as to pafs it by unnoticed, were flighting the merit of thofe by whofe means alone it has attained that eminence, it was Refolved, That the beft printed and moft correct Book which fhall be produced within a limited time be diftinguifhed by an honorary reward."*

They accordingly offered "a Silver Medal with a proper device and infcription" for the finest and most correct book " of at least ten fheets."† In April of the following year the reward was adjudged to Robert & Andrew Foulis for their folio edition of the Hymns of Callimachus.‡ Next year they obtained the Society's medal for their third edition of Horace as a Latin,—and their folio edition of Homer's Iliad as a Greek book. The last of these works is well known as one of the finest classics ever produced at any press. By the preface, it appears to have been printed at the expense of the professors in the University. It was intended as a trial, and in case of succeeding it was proposed to print all

---

* Scots Magazine, 1755, pp. 126, 7.

† Rules and Orders of the Society, pp. 24—5.

‡ Scots Magazine, 1756, p. 195. This edition was accompanied with engravings done at the Academy. They are not of any value, either for correctness of drawing or execution.

the Greek and Roman classics "with the fame elegance and accuracy." The text was taken from Dr. Clarke's quarto edition, published in 1729, and was collated with that of Henry Stephen's, which they imitated in the forms of the letters. They do not appear, however, to have followed Clarke in the accentuation, and the words are all printed at full length, in both which particulars their edition has been considered preferable.* After having been six times revised by different persons,† it was printed off in two folio volumes,—the small paper at the price of a guinea, and the large at a guinea and a half in sheets.

In 1758 the medal was again obtained for Foulis's edition of the Odyssey. The competing parties were not limited either to the form or number of sheets, the only conditions being that of the books offered in competition there should be at least two hundred and fifty copies printed for sale, and that the printers' name should be affixed to them.‡ In the following year the Glasgow edition of the minor works of Homer was declared the best specimen produced.|| During all this period the only successful rivals of the Foulises were Hamilton, Balfour, and Neill, of Edinburgh, who in 1758 gained a prize for their edition of Terence, got up under the care of the late Mr Alexander Smellie, at that time the corrector of their press.§

It was about this period (1757 or 1758) that Robert Foulis became acquainted with the late William Richardson, Esquire, afterwards professor of humanity in the College of Glasgow. With this elegant scholar he had much intercourse,—and it is to one of the papers Richardson left

---

* Monthly Review, October 1757.

† Twice by the corrector of Foulis's press,—then by Andrew Foulis,—by one of the editors, and afterwards twice by both.

‡ Scots Magazine, 1758, p. 44.

|| Ibid, 1759, p. 214.

§ Kerr's Life of Smellie, vol. i. p. 29.

behind him that we are principally indebted for the little knowledge we can now acquire of the personal history of the Foulises.

The book shop of the printers to the University was then, and for many years afterwards, within the precincts of the college ; and was at this time a place of resort with students, who either liked to talk about, or look at, books.* It was here that Foulis and Richardson first met.

It will, undoubtedly, appear to the reader a singular feature in Foulis's character, that he should choose to associate even with the youngest students, and to become a member of their literary clubs ; but this may be easily accounted for. Besides the gratification he had in displaying his sentiments upon literary and philosophical subjects, he believed that the knowledge he imparted, and the example he exhibited, might be useful to his juvenile auditors. Nothing could be more amusing or more interesting, according to Professor Richardson, than the literary discussions of the elder Foulis. In these, as he had a good deal of natural, though turbid, eloquence, he sometimes indulged at considerable length. The fashion of the times did not impose upon him a scrupulous attention to a restrained or castigated manner ; while his countenance, which indicated at once intellect and sensibility, and his frame, which was not of eminent stature, were often impressed with the vehemence of his oratory.†

To attempt any account of the Foulises during the following ten years, would in fact be only giving a dry detail of works printed at their press.

Towards the end of 1767, Dr Beattie, who appears by this time to have got acquainted with them, informs us that at Robert Foulis' request he had applied for, and obtained, from Gray, the poet, permission to

---

* Richardson's Letter, p. 1.
† Ibid, p. 6.

have an edition of his poems printed at Glasgow. Gray had before given Dodsley a similar permission;* and as the London bookseller had already gone to press, it was necessary that our Scotch printers should use all diligence. In reference to this subject, Dr Beattie writes thus to his friend Mr Arbuthnot:—

"The writing out a copy of Mr. Gray's Poems for the Prefs has occupied me the laſt fortnight. They are to be printed at Glaſgow by Foulis, with the author's own permiſſion, which I ſolicited and obtained: and he ſent me four folio pages of notes and additions to be inſerted in the new edition. The notes are chiefly illuſtrations of the two Pindaric Odes, more copious, indeed, than I ſhould have thought neceſſary, but I underſtand he is not a little chagrined at the complaints which have been made of their obſcurity; and he tells me, that he wrote theſe Notes out of ſpite. 'The long Story' is left out in this edition, at which I am not well pleaſed; for though it has neither head nor tail, beginning nor end, it abounds in humorous deſcription, and the verſification is exquiſitely fine. Three new Poems (never before printed) are inſerted, two of which are imitations from the Norwegian, and one is an imitation from the Welſh. He verſified them, he ſays, 'becauſe there is a wild ſpirit in them which ſtruck him.' From the firſt of the Norwegian pieces he has taken the hint of the *web*, in the Ode on the Welſh bards; but the imitation far exceeds the original. . . . . . I expect the book will be out in a few weeks, if Foulis be diligent, which it is his intereſt to be, as there is another edition of the ſame juſt now print-

---

* Gray to Dr Beattie, December 24th, 1767. Mason's Life of Gray, Letter 56. "I rejoice," says he, "to be in the hands of Mr. Foulis, who has the laudable ambition of ſurpaſſing his predeceſſors, the Etiennes and Elzevirs, as well in Literature, as in the proper art of his profeſſion."—Letter 57.

ing by Dodſley. I gave him notice of this, by Mr. Gray's defire, two months ago, but it did not in the leaſt abate his zeal for the undertaking."*

The Glasgow edition accordingly appeared about the middle of the same year in quarto,—" one of the moſt elegant pieces of Printing," says the author of the Minstrel," that the Glaſgow Prefs or any other Prefs has ever produced. It does honour to every perſon concerned in it,— to Mr. Foulis the Printer, and even to me the Publiſher, as well as to the Author."†

Contrary to the expectations, probably, of every one except Foulis himself, his edition was rapidly sold off, although Dodsley had before glutted the London market with two impressions, one of fifteen hundred, and the other of seven hundred and fifty copies, "both indeed far inferior to that of Glaſgow, but ſold at half the price."‡ Foulis found himself a considerable gainer, and was, to use Gray's expression, "magnificent in his gratitude." He offered his author a present of his Homer in four volumes folio, or the Greek Historians in twenty-nine volumes duodecimo,—the first of which seems to have been accepted.||

A folio edition of Milton's Poems (which appeared in 1770) seems next to have been proposed by our printers. This splendid work was published by subscription, and for some hints respecting it they were again indebted to the friendship of Beattie. The letter relating to it is one of the very few of Foulis' papers which have escaped destruction.— It is now printed for the first time.

---

* Beattie's Letters. Lond. 1820. vol. i. p. 47—9.
† Sir W. Forbes' Life of Dr Beattie, vol. i. p. 111. 8vo. edition.
‡ Gray to Dr Beattie, October 31st, 1768.
|| Ibid, July 16th, 1769.

ABERDEEN, *20th June*, 1770.

DEAR SIR,—I received your letter of the 10th of May, and about a fortnight after, the Books came to hand. The Milton is wonderfully fine. It is indeed the moſt magnificent Book I have ever ſeen, and ſeems to be perfectly correct. I am very happy to ſee that the hints I propoſ'd relating to Apoſtrophes have obtained your approbation. The omiſſion of thoſe unneceſſary characters has a very good effect on the eye, and will, I am convinced, give general satiſfaction. I hope you will ſoon ſet about Virgil in the ſame form. My former hints have been ſo well received, that I may poſſibly hazard a few on this ſubject alſo. I would not wiſh to ſee either the Culex or the Civis in this projected Edition, being thoroughly convinced that they are not by Virgil but by ſome much later hand. They are beſides altogether unworthy of the Mantuan bard. I could offer many arguments in proof of this opinion, but I flatter myſelf they will not be neceſſary. The Bucolics, Georgics, and Æneid are in my judgment the whole of Virgil's works now extant. I have two curious and, I believe, rare editions of this author: the firſt by Daniel Heinſius printed by Elzevir in the year 1636, and the other by his son Nicholas Heinſius printed by Elzevir in 1676. The laſt is by much the better, and is generally acknowledged to be the very beſt edition of Virgil. If you cannot find it elſewhere, my copy is at your ſervice. There are ſome various readings from the Medicean, and other Manuſcripts, which are of conſequence, and therefore ought not to be omitted in a correct edition of Virgil. In regard to theſe I have some written notes by me, which might probably be of ſome uſe. If you think ſo, I ſhall very readily communicate them. By the Bearer, Proſeſſor Traill, I have ſent payment of your account, viz, two guineas for Homer,—four and ſixpence for Epictetus, Anacreon and Cebes,— a guinea for Milton,—Two pounds thirteen Shillings for the Greek Hiſtorians,—and thirteen Shillings for my copy of Milton on ſmall paper, which you forgot to put into the account,—in all £6 : 13 : 6. I am much obliged to you for the concern you fhow about my Effay, and am very curious to know your opinion of it, and fhall be very happy if it obtains your approbation. The greateft merit of it is, that it is written with a good defign. It will offend many, but may I hope be of ufe to fome: nay, if I am not mifinformed, it has been so already. It was not without long confideration that I ventured it abroad in its prefent form. There is a boldnefs in many of the reflections, which after much thinking I thought it beft not to alter, though I hear it has given much offence to many of the Literati of your country. I have hardly time to add, that I truly am, Dear Sir, Your moft obedient Humble Serv[t.]

J. BEATTIE.

The edition of Virgil here mentioned never appeared.* The same determination which had prompted Foulis, contrary to all advice, to establish his Academy, had led him to continue it long after it might have been evident to himself, as it was to every one else, that it was embarrassing him in his operations as a printer, without the slightest probability of ultimate remuneration.

The prosperity of the Foulises may from this period be considered as on the decline, and the energy with which their business had been conducted seems now to have been completely wanting.† 'The Seven Cartoons of Raphael, formerly at Hampton Court, and now in the

---

* The Works of Virgil were printed by Andrew Foulis (Robert's Son) in two vols. folio, in 1778, "as a companion to Milton and Homer." (G. Paton to R. Gough, Esq. 21st December, 1778. MS. Adv. Lib.)

† "Foulis' conduct is unaccountable. (I) blufh at the breach of promife & bad treatment :—What need I fay? Many complain in the fame ftyle of them." (Geo. Paton to R. Gough, Esq. 28th September, 1772).

Queen's Palace,' appeared, indeed, in 1773, but they must be considered rather as one of the last efforts of their Academy than of their press. They continued to print for two years longer, till the death of Andrew, which took place on the 18th of September, 1775.* He had accompanied a stranger to the high ground adjoining the ancient residence of the family of Montrose, for the purpose of having a complete view of the city. He was here attacked by a apoplectic fit, and died almost immediately. Robert was sent for and had the body conveyed to his house, though from the suddenness of the event he could hardly be persuaded that his brother was dead. He hung over the body when it was stretched out, and called upon him again and again; but Andrew could make no reply.†

"The two Foulis[es]," says Dr Wodrow, "in fpite of their poverty and birth, were *par nobile fratrum*. I never indeed faw a more affectionate pair. They feem to have been made for one another. Though fimilar in their good difpofitions, they were totally oppofite in their genius or peculiar turn of mind. Neither of them, when feparated from the other, could have done much for himfelf or the world; but, like the members of the human body, 1 Cor. xii. 20, 21. & 9, or like the higher and lower orders in a community, they were admirably fitted by an all-directing Providence, by their conjunction and union, to do much in their ftation, for the honor of their country and the general improvement of Society."‡ Andrew had during their long and celebrated career laboured with the most slavish industry. After the commencement of the Academy, the superintendence of the printing, bookselling, and bookbinding departments of their business devolved upon him. Besides these, he had every evening in winter an auction of books.

---

* Scots Mag. 1775, p. 526.
† Richardson's Letter, p. 13.
‡ Letter from Dr Wodrow to the Earl of Buchan.

The accumulated cares which now pressed upon Robert Foulis, rendered it necessary that he should discontinue his labours in behalf of the Fine Arts. Besides his brother, Mr Archibald Ingram, who had along with those already mentioned * been a partner in the Academy since the 21st of February, 1758, was now dead, and the survivors were probably anxious to put a termination to an institution, which they had so long supported, not only without the remuneration they were entitled by their contract to insist upon, but at considerable loss.† There was now, besides, a Royal Academy in the metropolis of the British empire,—an institution which had risen with almost unprecedented rapidity.‡

As the most proper means of disposing of the collection of pictures, which had now become very numerous, it was determined that they should be brought to sale by auction. They were accordingly packed up and despatched to London, whither Robert Foulis himself, accompanied by Robert Dewar, one of his printers, also repaired. This person was afterwards married to one of Foulis' daughters, and it is but justice to his memory to say, that he seems to have entertained for

---

* See page 18. Mr Ingram died, July 23d, 1770. (Sederunt Book of his Trustees).

† By this contract Robert and Andrew Foulis became bound to pay to John Glassford of Dougalston, John Campbell, and Archibald Ingram, £40 a year each. (List of R. and A. Foulis' Debts.) The sums for which these gentlemen became liable, amounted (after deduction) to about £1140.

‡ The present Royal Academy was instituted in 1768, and was to be supported by the produce of annual exhibitions, the deficiency (if any) being supplied out of his Majesty's Privy Purse. For a few years it required his Majesty's aid, but as the exhibitions became every year more productive, they were more than sufficient for the support of the establishment. The exhibitions from 1769 to 1780 produced on an average £1500 annually, and from that time to 1796 about £2500. (Malone's Life of Sir J. Reynolds, prefixed to his Works, p. 39).

his master a high degree of respect, and to have watched over him, when at length overtaken by sickness, with an almost filial anxiety.

They arrived in London about the month of April, 1776, but here new calamities awaited them. Before the pictures could be prepared for exhibition, the season was too far advanced. "All the people of rank," says Foulis in his last letter to his son, " or at leaft the generality, are out of the Town, and the Exhibition is dwindled even to lefs than what it was. I know no expedient that can be tried to help it but one,— fhowing them for nothing, and taking 6d. for the Catalogue : this expedient might do, were it not for the difficulty of making it known, becaufe Advertifements are fo little read, and fo many of them to read, that a confiderable expence gone for Advertifing produces but a very little effect. . . . . . . The run of the exhibitions are already over. It is very mortifying to me to be obliged to fee this expedition a load on the Company : this has happened fo independent of all choice, that I could no more help it, than remove mountains ; but when better fortune comes, I will remember it."*

Notwithstanding these discouragements, and contrary to the advice of Christie, the auctioneer,† the pictures were sold off, and as might have been expected, at a grevious disadvantage. Whether Foulis had overestimated the value of his pictures, or depended too much on the friendship and patronage of those on whom he thought he had some claim, are questions it would now be difficult to answer. Professor Richardson, however, has stated from authority, on which he felt disposed to rely, that a picture, sold for twenty-five pounds, afterwards brought five hundred.‡ Two of the paintings belonging to the Academy were pur-

---

* This Letter, which is among Lord Buchan's Papers, is dated "London, May 2. 1776."
† Foulis's Letter to Campbell, Glassford, and Ingram, Orig. Pap. No. VI.
‡ Richardson's Letter, p. 20.

chased by the University, and are now in their possession. One of them was considered by so good a judge as the late Sir Henry Raeburn to have been the production, if not of Raphael himself at an early period, at least of one of his scholars.*

Foulis's mortification, amounting even to resentment, from the failure of this last hope, was the more acute as it had naturally no place in his sanguine disposition. He thought himself neglected where he expected attention, and ill-used where he looked for favour. It is honourable to the memory of one, however, to whom the University of Glasgow, and the Scottish literati generally, have been much indebted, to be enabled to state, that his kindness to Foulis in this situation of his affairs was unabated,—this person was the celebrated Dr William Hunter. He had been at an early period indebted to Foulis for an introduction to Dr Douglas of London, and his gratitude does not seem to have diminished, when success in his profession,—the closeness of his application to it,— and the distance from Scotland, might almost have rendered it probable. During this trying period he made every effort to support the mind of his aged and unfortunate friend :—he even hinted that a certain great personage might probably visit his exhibition. This however not having taken place as he wished, Hunter repeated his hopes of it :—" It does not fignify," said Foulis, with a look of independent unconcern, " I fhall foon be in the prefence of the King of kings."

But little of this melancholy story remains to be told. With the feelings already described, and with a constitution nearly exhausted, Foulis left London. He reached Edinburgh, and while in the act of preparing for his journey to Glasgow, suddenly expired on the 2d of June, 1776.†

---

* Richardson's Letter, p. 20.
† Scots Magazine, June, 1776. Richardson, p. 19

From the different facts noticed in the course of this sketch, the reader may have been enabled to form some estimate of the character of Robert Foulis. To complete the outline, the following notices, by Professor Richardson, may not be uninteresting :—

"The firſt feature in Robert Foulis' charaƈter, that particularly ſtruck me, was the great liking he ſhowed to converſe on literary topics, and even with perſons much younger than himſelf. This diſpoſition appeared not only in occaſional interviews, but in his chooſing to aſſociate with them, and become a member of their Literary Clubs and Societies. This view of his charaƈter, which appeared to me ſingular, was in my apprehenſion rendered particularly intereſting by that unſuſpeƈting goodwill and benignity of diſpoſition with which it was intimately united. For, beſides the gratification he had, and no doubt he had a great deal, in diſplaying his own ſentiments and opinions on ſubjeƈts of Taſte, the Fine Arts, Literature, and even Theology, he likewiſe believed, and had reaſon to believe, that the knowledge he imparted, and the example he exhibited, might be uſeful to his juvenile auditors. It will readily occur that ſuch diſpoſitions & habits muſt have been prompted and induced by great fervor of mind, and, in truth, there was no inconſiderable ſhare of enthuſiaſm, but unaccompanied with any peculiar impropriety, in his ſentiments and even in his conduƈt. (Though he was ardent he was ſeldom incenſed, and his eagerneſs, or rather earneſtneſs, was never keen.) His good ſenſe and natural flow of affeƈtion and complacency allayed at that period* of his life every riſing impulſe of animoſity ; ſo that every ſudden diſpleaſure he ever felt, ſuch as may be incidental to perſons of ſenſibility, was, in the calm of a benignant and forgiving temper, very ſoon and completely aſſuaged. Thus diſpoſed and united, and being a warm admirer of the ſublime and affeƈting repreſentations preſented by

---

* The period at which Richardson became acquainted with him. See page 31.

the Poet and the Painter, his religion was nearly allied to that of Fenelon, and his Philoſophy was akin to the opinions, as he ſuppoſed, of Plato, or the more intelligible Doƈtrines of Cicero. Such indeed were the ſentiments which he often enforced in his difcuffions in thoſe Literary and Philoſophical Clubs and Societies, in which he uſually bore a part." He was rather below the middle fize, yet perfeƈtly well-proportioned, and his whole appearance indicated a ſtrong and robuſt conſtitution. His complexion had not much colour, but was fair, and the habitual expreffion of his countenance was that of an amiable and good-hearted difpoſition.*

There were occasions in which the character of Robert Foulis appeared in rather an amusing point of view. The brothers, as has been already mentioned, had every evening during winter an auction of books. Andrew generally officiated as auctioneer, but if prevented from attending, his brother took his place. On these occasions when a book was presented to him for sale, he not only announced the title, but on many occasions continued an extemporaneous harangue upon its contents. His candour prevented him from uniformly praising the book. When "the History of Tom Jones" was one night handed to him, "How," said he, with considerable warmth, " was this book presented ? It is improper for the perusal of young persons." And having said this, he returned it to the clerk. On another occasion, having observed a student, whose appearance did not indicate a superabundance of the good things of this world, offer several times for a copy of Antoninus, he asked whether he was anxious to have it. Being answered in the affirmative, he presented it to him.

But such opportunities of displaying his generosity, were not often afforded him. For his brother, aware of his propensities, hastened to

---

* Richardson's Letter, pp. 2, 3, 6.

disengage himself, and exerting, partly in jest and partly in earnest, an authority which on other occasions he rarely claimed, "Come down," he would say, "Robin, that place and that buisness are not for you." And thus was he dismissed from his employment.*

No work is known to have been written by either of the Foulises, except "the Catalogue of Pictures," with critical and explanatory remarks by the elder.† This, however, must not be regarded as a fair specimen of his talents. It was written hurriedly with the immediate view to their being sold in London,—when the author was sixty-eight years of age,—and soon after his brother's death. He had, besides, been severely tried by family afflictions; for having been twice married he survived both wives and several of his daughters.‡ The criticism of Professor Richardson regarding this work is perfectly just. It is too circumstantial,—too minute in many of the descriptions, and consequently too much spun out. Yet with all this, it wants many things essential to a work of that kind. The pictures, we are told, are painted by Raphael, Guido, Michael Angelo, and others, but nothing is said of their history,—how they were obtained,—nor is any evidence brought

---

* Richardson's Letter, p. 9.

† Several " Prefaces by the Publishers " are prefixed to the works they printed.

‡ Foulis married first in September, 1742, Elizabeth Moor, daughter of James Moor, teacher of mathematics in Glasgow, and sister to the celebrated Grecian. This lady (by whom he had five daughters), having gone to Edinburgh in 1750 to visit some of her relations, was suddenly seized with an illness, which carried her off in a few weeks. Foulis's grief on this occasion was so great, that Dr Black had to drag him by force from the room in which the body lay. [Mrs Dewar to E. of Buchan.] He married secondly, a Miss Boutcher, daughter of William Boutcher, seedsman in Edinburgh, and author of a "Treatise on Forest Trees," published, according to Paton, "by subscription, as much for the benefit of the author as for the merit of the work, *tho' it's said not to be amiss.*" —(Correspondence with Gough 29th December, 1775, Adv. Lib.) From this lady, the late Andrew Foulis descended.

forward to prove that they are genuine.* The course of Foulis' education had never led him to the study of elegance or accuracy in composition; in this respect also the work will be found deficient. Yet it displays the remains of what all who knew him acknowledged him to possess,—" original genius."† It exhibits on several occasions an intimate knowledge of the subject, and great correctness and delicacy of moral and philosophical discrimination.

As senior member, it was Robert Foulis's turn to read a discourse to the Literary Society at their first meeting for the winter 1776, but lest he should not have been able to return from London before that time, another was appointed in his stead. His substitute opened the business of the Society in the following words,—alike honourable to the feelings of the speaker, and the memory of his departed friend.

" When I promifed, a few months ago, to begin the bufinefs of the Society for the prefent feffion, I entertained expectations that the fulfilment of my engagement would not have been required of me. A venerable member was then living, though at that time abfent from his home, never indeed to return, to whom that office would have fallen of courfe. He is no longer a member of this Society, or of any fociety of mortal men; he is gone whither all of us fhall fooner or later follow, and happy may we deem our departure, if we leave behind us a name like his. I am well perfuaded, indeed, that our remembering him on the prefent occafion will not be unpleafant. We have often feen him in this Society, entering with ardour into every ingenious and important difcuffion. But I fay nothing of the gratitude due to him by every lover

---

* Richardson's Letter, pp. 25, 26.

† Dr Wodrow, writing of Foulis, calls him "a man of original genius, of a very liberal and enlarged mind, and of a moft benevolent difinterefted fpirit." (Letter to the Earl of Buchan, May, 1808.)

of true learning, and of claffical elegance. It is not my purpofe to pronounce his panegyric, for his eulogy is eftablifhed on a firmer foundation than any memorial of mine. As long as the luminaries of Greece and of Rome are held in eftimation, will his fame be remembered, and when *they* cease to be valued, who would choofe to be named? (True, no doubt, ages have arifen in the hiftory of mankind that give them no glory, but they were ages of darknefs and had no glory to give). Nor will I enumerate his virtues. I only mean to recall him to your remembrance, for furely he deferves well of us all. His public fpirit embracing the welfare and improvement of this community, and indeed of the human kind, was accompanied, even in old age, with all the ardour of private affection, and all the enthufiafm of youthful friendfhip. Bending with years, and fully aware that a change in his mortal nature was faft approaching, and that he was no longer to have any concern in the affairs of men, he entered warmly into their interefts, and preferved till his lateft hour zealous wifhes for their improvement. Few fpeak of the dead: they lie filent and forgotten. Yet it is no unbecoming exercife to renew the memory of a worthy friend. It is often no lefs profitable than the converfe of the living, and often no lefs delightful. I truft that I have obtruded no difagreeable remembrances on my audience: at leaft for my part I have fome claim for indulgence."*

From the facts which have beeen already mentioned, the reader will not be surprised to find that the affairs of Robert and Andrew Foulis were left in a state of insolvency. It must be matter of deep regret that the zeal with which they prosecuted whatever might promote the

---

* Richardson's Letter, pp. 26, 27, 28. The name of the speaker is not mentioned.

literature and arts of their country, should have been so indifferently rewarded. Persons of less enterprise might have risen to affluence from the decided superiority of their printing; but Robert Foulis's family was left in almost complete destitution. Their affairs were finally wound up in 1781, by Robert Chapman, printer, and James Duncan, bookseller in Glasgow. Their debts amounted to rather more than six thousand five hundred pounds, and nearly the whole of their stock was purchased by Mr James Spottiswood of Edinburgh.

CATALOGUE OF BOOKS.

CATALOGUE OF BOOKS.

[*The following List comprehends not only the Works executed by Urie for Robert Foulis, and those printed by the latter individually, but also the joint productions of the two brothers.*]

1741.

1. The Temper, Character, and Duty of a Minifter of the Gofpel. A Sermon preached before the Synod of Glafgow and Ayr, at Glafgow, April 7th, 1741. By William Leechman, A.M. Minifter of Beith, 8vo.
2. Cicero de Natura Deorum. Accedunt Bouherii, Davifii, et aliorum infigniores lectiones variantes et conjecturæ, 8vo.
3. Phædri Fabulæ, ex editione Burmanni, 12mo.
4. Bifhop Burnet's Life of John, Earl of Rochefter, 12mo.
5. A Catechifm, or an Inftruction in the Chriftian Religion by way of Queftion and Anfwer, &c. By Rev. John Mears, A.M., 8vo.
6. Leechman's Sermon, second edition, 8vo.

1742.

7. Juvenalis et Perfii Satyræ, fools. 8vo.
8. Philofophiæ Moralis Inftitutio Compendiaria, Ethices et Jurifprudentiæ Naturalis Elementa continens, Libri Tres. Auctore Francifco Hutchefon in Academia Glafguenfi, P. P. 12mo.
9. Metaphyficæ Synopfis, Ontologiam et Pneumatologiam complectens, 8vo.
10. The Meditations of M. Aurelius Antoninus. Newly Tranflated from the Greek : with Notes and an Account of his Life, 12mo.

The two first books by Professor Moor, and the rest by Dr Francis Hutcheson.

11. The State of Religion in New England fince the Rev. Mr. George Whitefield's arrival there, &c. first and second editions, 8vo.
12. An Impartial Trial of the Spirit operating in this part of the World; by comparing the nature, effects, and evidences of the prefent fuppofed converfion with the Word of God : A Sermon preached at New Londonderry, October 4th, 1741. By John Caldwell, A. M. Bofton printed. Reprinted by Robert Foulis, 8vo.
13. A Zeal for good Works excited and directed : in a Sermon at the public Thurfday Lecture in Bofton, March 25th, 1742. By John Bernard, A. M. &c. 8vo.
14. P. Terentii Afri Comœdiæ, Ex editione Westerhoviana, 12mo. and 8vo.
   "On Fine Paper, 3s. 6d. bound : 12mo. coarfer paper at 1s. 3d. bound, and forty copies are printed on a grand Royal Paper at 8s." This accounts for Dibdin's mistake in supposing that all other copies except those on royal paper are common. —Introd. to Classics, second edition. Vol. i. p. 476.
15. The Wonderful Narrative : or a Faithful Account of the French Prophets, their agitations, exftafies, and infpirations, &c. 8vo.
16. Hales on Religion, 12mo.
17. Leechman's Sermon, third edition, 8vo.
18. Burnet's Select Sermons, 8vo.

1743.

19. More's Utopia. Tranflated by Bifhop Burnet, 8vo.
20. Instructions to a Son, containing Rules of Conduct in Public and Private Life, &c. By Archibald, Marquis of Argyle, 12mo.
21. Demetrius Phalereus de Elocutione, Gr. et Lat., crown 8vo. 1s.
   "A few are printed off in 4to. on a fine Paper."
22. Divine Dialogues, containing Difquifitions concerning the Attributes and Providence of God. By Henry More, D. D., 3 vols. 12mo.
23. The Nature, Reafonablenefs, and Advantages of Prayer. With an attempt to anfwer the Objections againft it. A Sermon by W. Leechman, A. M., Minifter of Beith, 8vo.
24. The Judgment of Hercules, 8vo. pp. 28.
25. The Confirming Work of Religion, or its great things made plain by their primary Evidences and Demonftrations, &c. By the late

Rev. Mr. Robert Fleming, author of "The fulfilling of the Scriptures," 18mo.

26. A Defcription of the Confirmed State of Chriftians. By the fame author, 18mo.
27. Theophrafti Chara&eres Ethici : ex recenfione Petri Needham, et cum verfione Latina Ifaaci Cafauboni, 8vo.
28. Boffuet's Account of the Education of the Dauphine, in a Letter to Pope Innocent XI. Tranflated by J. T. Phillips, Preceptor to H. R. H. Prince William Duke of Cumberland, fools. 12mo. 1d.

1744.

29. Quinti Horatii Flacci Opera, 12mo.
    Fine paper small 8vo. The immaculate edition.—See page 14.
30. Antoninus de Se ipfo, Gr. et Lat. cum notis R. J. 2 vols. small 8vo.
31. Ciceronis Difputationes Tufculanæ cum le&ionibus variantibus et Cl. Bouherii conje&uris, 12mo.
32. Epi&eti Manuale, Cebetis Tabula, Prodicus et Cleanthes, Gr. et Lat., 12mo.
33. Epi&eti Enchiridion Latinis Verfibus Adumbratum per Edvardum Ivie, A. M. &c., 12mo.
34. Leechman's Sermon, fourth edition, 8vo.
35. Anacreontis et Sapphonis Carmina, Gr. et Lat. 12mo.
36. Pindari Opera, 2 vols. Gr. et Lat., fools. 8vo, fine, 3s. 6d. common 2s.
    "I have carefully read this edition twice through, and affirm it to be one of the moft accurate of the Glafgow editions of the Greek claffics."—Harwood, pp. 8, 9.
37. Synopfis Metaphyficæ, Ontologiam et Pneumatologiam comple&ens. Editio fecunda, demy 12mo.
38. Plutarchus de Superftitione, Xenophontis Socrates, et Ariftodemus de Providentia : Platonis Alcibiades Secundus de Numine Orando. Gr. et Lat., 12mo.
    Some copies bear the name of Robert only,—others those of R. & A. Foulis. There is little doubt, however, that Robert must be considered responsible for the inaccuracies which this volume contains, as the preface begins "*Typographus Junioribus Academicis.*" The correcting of the press had been left entirely to the compositor, and in reading it over after it was printed, so many errors were dis-

covered that it was allowed to remain unpublished for about twelve years. The date of publication was April, 1756, and even then it was intended only "In ufum Juventutis Academicæ."—See Pref. The propriety of giving an inaccurate book into the hands of a student may be questioned.

1745.

39. Smith on the Noblenefs and Excellency of True Religion, 8vo.
40. Sophoclis Tragœdiæ; cum verfione Latina et lectionibus variantibus, 2 vols. fools. 8vo.

> "One of the moft incorrect of the Glafgow Greek claffics. In carefully reading this edition feveral times through, I have difcovered and corrected above an hundred inaccuracies. It is beautifully printed."—Harwood, p. 13.

41. The fame, Gr. fools. 4to.

> "An excellent edition."—Harwood, p. 12.

42. Xenophontis Hiero, Gr. et Lat. fools. 8vo. 6d.
43. Ariftotelis Poetica, Gr. et Lat. cum lectionibus variantibus, fools. 8vo.
44. Ariftotelis de Mundo Liber, Gr. et Lat. crown 12mo. 3d.
45. Hutchefoni Philofophiæ Moralis Inftitutio Compendiaria. Editio altera auctior et emendatior.

1746.

46. True Religion, a Myftery, 8vo.
47. Guardian, 2 vols. 12mo.
48. Æfchyli Tragœdia, cum verfione Latina et lectionibus variantibus, 2 vols. fools. 8vo. common, 3s.
49. Idem liber, Gr. fools. 4to. cum lectionibus variantibus, 6s.

> "An edition much more correct than the fmall one publifhed at Glafgow the fame year, in 2 vols. 12mo., though this laft is a refpectable edition; for, in reading it four times through, I have only difcovered about ten inaccuracies of any moment."—Harwood, p. 11.

50. The Cherrie and the Slae, compylit into Scottis Meeter, by Captain Alexander Montgomery. Firft printed MDXCVII., by Robert Waldegrave, printer to King James VI. 12mo.
51. Letters to the Duke of Burgundy, by M. de Fenelon, Archbifhop of Cambray, demy 4to. 3d. fools. 4to. 2½d. pot 4to. 2d.
52. Theocriti Opera, Gr. fools. 4to. fine, 4s. 6d. common, 3s.
53. The fame, Gr. and Lat. fools. 8vo. fine, 2s. 6d. common, 2s.

1747.

54. Homeri Ilias, Gr. 2 vols. fools. 4to. 6s.
55. The fame, Gr. and Lat. 2 vols. fools. 8vo. common, 2s. 6d.
    On the blank side of the last page :—" Excudebatur apud Fratres Robertum et Andream Foulis Academiæ Glafguenfi Typographos. Anno MDCCXLVII pridie Nonas Septembris." A few 8vo. copies were thrown off on vellum, of which three remained in 1777. The trade price of the latter seems to have been 10s. in sheets.
56. Longinus.
57. Cebetis Tabula. Accedit Interpretatio Latina ex Editione J. Gronovii. 12mo.
    "Very beautiful and accurate."—Harwood, p. 22.
58. Hutcheson's Compend of Moral Philofophy, [in Englifh] fools. 12mo. 1s. 6d.
59. Tatler, 4 vols. fools. 8vo. fine, 7s. 6d.
60. Relph's Poems, 8vo.

1748.

61. The Philofophical Principles of Natural and Revealed Religion, unfolded in Geometrical order. By the Chevalier Ramfay, Author of the Travels of Cyrus. 2 vols. writing demy, 4to. 21s. fools. 4to. 10s. 6d.
    Some copies are marked, London, 1749—51.
62. Cicero de Officiis.
63. An Effay on the Compofition and Manner of Writing of the Ancients, particularly Plato. By the late James Geddes, Efq. Advocate, demy 8vo. With a Life of the Author, by William Leechman, D.D. Principal of the Univerfity of Glafgow, 3s.
64. Xenophontis de Agefilao Rege Oratio. Adjecta eft verfio Latina ex editione T. Hutchefon, 8vo.
65. The battles of Hairlaw and the Reid Squire. Two Old Hiftorical Scots Poems, fools. 8vo. fine, 2d. common, 1d.
66. Hippocratis Aphorifmi, Gr. et Lat. 12mo.
67. Hardyknute, fools. 4to. fine 3d.
    A List of the different editions of Hardyknute is given in the 2d vol. (p. 16.) of the Letters to Mr George Paton, edited by James Maidment, Esq. a Member of the Club.

68. Poems in the Scottiſh Dialect, by ſeveral celebrated Poets : viz. Chriſt's Kirk, Habbie Simſon and Sanny Brig's Elegies, The Blythſome Wedding, Kennedy's Teſtament, Johnie Armſtrang, a Satyre on Covetouſneſs, Panegyric on Sir Penny, Robin and Makyne, Interlude of the Droichs, an Epiſtle, 8vo. pp. 48.
69. Epicteti Enchiridion, Ex Editione J. Upton accurate expreſſum, Gr. et Lat. 12mo.
70. Ciceronis Orator, 18mo.

1749.

71. Apollonii Pergæi Locorum Planorum, Libri II. Reſtituti a Roberto Simſon, M.D. 4to.
72. Poems on Several Occaſions, [by William Hamilton, Eſq. of Bangour,] 12mo.
73. Lucretius de Rerum Natura. Sine notis, 8vo.
74. Antoninus, [Engliſh] 2 vols. 8vo. second edition.
75. The Original, Nature and Immortality of the Soul, a Poem by Sir J. Davies, 12mo.
76. Cornelius Nepos, fools. 8vo.
77. Synopſis Metaphyſicæ, third edition, 8vo.
78. M. Tullii Ciceronis Opera quæ ſuperſunt omnia, 20 vols. fools. 12mo. fine, 40s., middle, 25s., common, 17s.

"The text of this very beautiful edition of Cicero, publiſhed at Glaſgow, is taken from Olivet, and is very correctly printed."—Harwood, p. 162. Price,—"£1 : 17 : 6. to Subſcribers in Sheets."—Scots Mag.

79. Propoſals for Printing by Subſcription the whole Works of Plato.

A letter from the celebrated John Wilkes to Robert Foulis, relative to the intended work, has been preserved.—It is now printed for the first time.

LONDON, *December 3d*, 1746.

SIR,—About a month ago, Mr. Dalrymple communicated to me ſome propoſals of yours for the Printing of Plato in ten Volumes Octavo, which he ſaid you would undertake if you were aſſured of a hundred ſubſcriptions at two gunieas each. I have ſince mentioned this to Mr Profeſſor Ward of Greſham College and to ſeveral other friends, who are very willing to encourage ſo uſeful a deſign; and I am deſired to write to you, to beg you would ſend us printed propoſals. We may venture to aſſure you of one hundred ſubſcriptions from the circle of **our own** acquaintance. This would be a trifling expence to you, as I imagine you would give the letter and paper of your 8vo. Sophocles for a fpecimen. It would be the greateft honour to your prefs, to print fo noble an author with as few errata as poffible; and you would benefit the learned world beyond what Stephens or Aldus ever did. The text of Servanus in general you will chufe I make no doubt; and if I might advife you, it would be to publifh firft the moft ftriking pieces of Plato, and the two or three firft volumes feparately. By this means every body would purchafe the firft volumes for the intrinfick excellency of the pieces, and the remaining volumes to complete their sets. I think you fhould begin with the Phædo, the Crito, and the two Alcibiades, then the Apology of Socrates, Timæus, the Sympofium, and Minon. You need not doubt the happy fale of thefe, and this would affure fuccefs to the whole work. If you approve of this, and chufe to undertake it, I fhould be obliged to you if you would anfwere this as foon as you can, and pleafe to direct to me in St John's Square, Clerkenwell.

I am, your humble fervant,

JOHN WILKES.

"This letter of Wilkes'," says the Earl of Buchan, "does more credit to his memory than the whole of his political career, tho' no friend to truth can deny that he was bafely perfecuted by the firft of thofe abominable adminiftrations that have difgraced the prefent reign [George III.], and brought Britain to the brink of ruin and deftruction."

1750.

80. Law on Money and Trade, 12mo.
81. C. Julii Cæfaris et A. Hirtii de rebus a Cæfare geftis Commentarii, fools. folio, 10s.
82. The fame, fools. 4to. 8s.
83. The fame, 3 vols. fools. 12mo. 1s. 9d.
84. Marci Minucii Felicis Octavius, ex recenfione Johannis Davifii, 4to.
85. The fame, 8vo.
86. Demofthenis Orationes Philippicæ, Gr. et Lat. fools. 8vo. fine, 2s. 6d., common, 1s. 6d.
87. De optimo Reipublicæ Statu, deque Nova Infula Utopia Libri II. Auctore Thoma More Equite, &c. Ex prioribus editionibus collatis accurate expreffi, 12mo.
88. The Trade and Navigation of Great Britian confidered. By Jofhua Gee, 12mo.

89. Milton's Paradife Loft, Book I. [with notes by John Callander, Efq. of Craigforth.] 4to. 1s. 6d.

> For some account of these notes, see Transactions of the Society of Scottish Antiquaries, vol. 3d. part I.

90. Demofthenes de Pace Cherfonefi, fools. 8vo.
91. Horatii Opera, editio altera [secunda] 8vo.
92. Anacreon, Sappho et Alcæus, Gr. fools. 8vo.
93. The Difpenfary, a Poem, in Six Cantos, by Sir Samuel Garth, 12mo.
94. The Manuel of Epictetus, containing an Abridgment of his Philofophy. Tranflated from the Greek, by George Stanhope, D.D. &c. pot' 12mo. common, 1½d.
95. The Banquet of Xenophon. Tranflated by Dr Wellwood, fools. 8vo. 1s. 2d.
96. Fenelon's Inftructions for the Education of Daughters. Tranflated by Hickes, 8vo.
97. Juvenalis et Perfii Satyræ, 8vo.
98. Baxter's Call, [in Gælic] fools. 8vo.
99. Musæus' Hero and Leander. Tranflated by L. Eufden, 8vo.
100. Fenelon's Letter to the French Academy concerning Rhetoric, Poetry, Hiftory, and a comparifon between the Antients and Moderns, fools. 8vo. 6d.
101. A Letter on occafion of the late Earthquakes, from the Lord Bifhop of London, to the Clergy and People of London and Weftminfter. Price Threepence. 12mo.
102. Dunbar's Thiftle and Rofe, 8vo.
103. Bellenden's Vertue and Vyce, 8vo.
104. Hutchefon on Laughter.
105. Milton's Paradife Loft, 8vo.
106. Ramfay's Gentle Shepherd, 12mo.
107. Gray's Fables, pot. 8vo. common, 6d.
108. Gray's Beggar's Opera.
109. Phædra and Hippolitus, a Tragedy. By Edmund Smith, Efq.
110. Love of Fame the Univerfal Paffion. By Dr Edward Young.
111. Drummond's Polemo-Middinia, 8vo.

112. Fenelon on Dejection of Mind, with the Remedys of Diffipation. fools. 8vo. fine, 3d.

1751.

113. Longinus de Sublimitate, Gr. et Lat. fine notis 8vo.
114. A Kempis de Imitatione Chrifti, 12mo. fools. fine 1s. 6d. common 1s.
115. Phædri Fabulæ, ex recenfione Burmanni, 8vo.
116. Propofals and Reafons for conftituting a Council of Trade, in Scotland, by the celebrated John Law of Lauriefton, pot 8vo. common 1s. 6d.
117. Sir William Petty's Political Arithmetic, 12mo.
118. The Force of Religion or Vanquifhed Love, a Poem in Two Books, [by Dr Edward Young] fools. 8vo. common 1d.
119. Lucanus, ex editione Burmanni.
120. Letter of Confolation to the Countefs of Effex on the lofs of her only Daughter, by Sir William Temple, fools. 8vo. fine, $2\frac{1}{2}$.
121. Poems on Moral and Divine Subjects, by feveral celebrated Englifh Poets, viz. Spencer, Ben Johnfon, &c. &c. 8vo.
122. Salluftii Opera ex recenfione Cortii, 8vo.
123. Sir Jofiah Child on Trade, pot 8vo. common 1s.
124. Pope's Effay on Man.
125. Nettleton's Treatife on Virtue and Happinefs.
126. Letters of Abelard to Heloife ; with the Hiftory of their Lives. Tranflated by Hughes, fools. 8vo. fine, 1s. 6d.
127. Xenophon's Difcourfe upon Improving the Revenue of the State of Athens. Tranflated from the Greek, by Walter Moyle, Efq. firft printed in the year 1679, 12mo.
128. Denham's Poems, pot 8vo. common 1s.
129. Poems on Several Occafions, by Jofeph Addifon, Efq.
130. Berkley's Queritt, 12mo.

The following Plays by Congreve :—

131. The Mourning Bride, a Tragedy.
132. The Way of the World, a Comedy.
133. The Judgement of Paris, a Mafque.

134. Semele, an Opera.
135. The Old Bachelor, a Comedy.
136. The Double Dealer, a Comedy.
137. Love for Love, a Comedy.
138. C. Plinii Cæcilii Secundi Epiſtolarum Libri X. et Panegyricus, 4to.
139. The same, 2 vols. 12mo.
140. Elements of Natural Philoſophy. By John Locke, Eſq.
141. The Tragedy of Cleopatra. By Mr Samuel Daniel.
142. The Conſcious Lovers. By Sir Richard Steele.
143. Scougal's Life of God in the Soul of Man, and Archbiſhop Leighton's Rules for a Holy Life.
144. Poems on Several Occaſions. By Mr. John Gay, 2 vols.
145. The Defects and Danger of a Phariſaical Righteouſneſs. A Sermon preached at Glaſgow, July 7th, 1751. By John Duncan, M.A. Chaplain to Col. Rich's Regiment, fools. 8vo. fine, 2d.
146. The Speech of a Fife Laird newly come from the Grave; the Mare of Collingtoun; the Baniſhment of Poverty; three Scots Poems, 8vo.
147. Montgomery's Cherrie and Slae, and other poems, crown, 8vo. fine, 9d., common, 4½d.
148. Boetius de Conſolatione Philoſophiæ, fools. 8vo. fine 1s. 6d.
149. The same, 4to.
"A correct edition."—Harwood, p. 220.
150. Epictetus, Gr. fools. 32mo. 9d.
"A very correct and beautiful book."—Harwood, p. 61.

1752.

151. Comparative Theology, or the True and Solid Grounds of Pure and Peaceable Theology, &c. fools. 12mo. fine, 4½d. common, 3d.
152. Milton's Paradiſe Loſt, 12mo.
153. The ſame, Regained, 12mo.
154. A Diſcourſe Concerning Natural and Revealed Religion. By Stephen Nye. Firſt printed in the year 1696, 12mo.

155. Poetæ Latini Minores ex Editione Burmanni fideliter expreffi, fools. 8vo. fine, 1s. 6d., common, 1s.
156. The Lutrin, an Heroi-Comical Poem, in Six Cantos, by Monfieur Boileau, &c. Fourth edition, fools. 8vo. common, 3d. fine, 4d.
157. Poems on Several Occafions. To which are added, the Tragedies of Julius Cæfar and Marcus Brutus. By John Sheffield, Duke of Buckingham, fools. 8vo. fine, 1s. 6d.
158. C. V. Paterculi Hiftoria ex Editione Burmanni fideliter expreffa, fools. 8vo. fine, 1s. 6d., common, 1s. 2d.
159. Poems on Several Occafions. By William Congreve, pot 8vo., common, 9d.
160. Fenelon's Dialogues of the Dead and Fables, 2 vols. 8vo. fine, 2s. 3d.
161. St Real's Hiftory of the Confpiracy of the Spaniards againft Venice in 1618, fools. 18mo. fine, 6d., common 4d.
162. Antoninus' Meditations, [Englifh] Third edition, 8vo.
163. Young's Laft Day, 8vo.
164. Lanfdowne's Plays, 8vo.
165. Pomponius Mela de Situ Orbis ex recenfione Gronovii, fools. 8vo. fine, 1s. 6d.
166. Locke on the Human Underftanding Abridged, 12mo.
167. Addifon's Plays.
168. Midfummer Night's Dream, by Shakefpear.
169. The Tempeft, by Shakefpear.
170. Aurenge-Zebe: or the Great Mogul, a Tragedy by John Dryden, Efq. 12mo.
171. Poems on Several Occafions. By Matthew Prior, Efq. 2 vols. fools, 8vo. 2s.
172. The Works of Edmund Waller, Efq. in Verfe and Profe. Publifhed by Mr. Fenton, fools. 8vo. fine, 1s.
173. Burnet's Life of the Earl of Rochefter, 12mo.
174. Dryden's Fables, Ancient and Modern, 2 vols. 12mo.
175. Venice Preferved, a Tragedy, 8vo.
176. The Sophy, a Tragedy, 8vo.
177. The Diftreft Mother, a Tragedy, 8vo.

1753.

178. Addifon on the Chriftian Religion, fools. 8vo. fine, 4½. common, 2½.
179. The Works of the Right Honorable Dillon Wentworth, Earl of Rofcommon, fools. 8vo., fine, 1s. 6d., common, 1s. 2d.
180. Æthiopian Adventures: or the Hiftory of Theagenes and Chariclea, written originally in Greek, by Heliodorus, &c. fools. 8vo. fine, 2s., common, 1s. 4d.
181. C. Cornelii Taciti Opera quæ Superfunt, ex Editione Gronovii fideliter expreffa. 4 vols. fools. 12mo. fine, 5s. 6d., common, 3s. 6d.
182. Aminta di Taffo. con figure, 12mo.
183. Tibulli et Propertii Opera ex editione Broukhufii fideliter expreffa, fools. 8vo. fine, 1s. 9d., common, 1s. 2d.
184. Plutarchi Chæronenfis de Audiendis Poetis cum interpretatione Grotii, variantes lectiones et notas adjecit Joannes Potter. Oxoniæ, 1694. fools. 8vo. fine, 1s. 9d., common, 1s. 2d.
185. Sure Methods of Attaining a Long and Healthful Life. By Lewis Cornaro, fools. 12mo. fine, 6d.
186. Hutchefon's Compend of Moral Philofophy, [Englifh,] fecond edition.
187. Merchant of Venice.
188. Love's Labour Loft.
189. The Life and Death of King Lear.
190. The Two Gentlemen of Verona.
191. The Merry Wives of Windfor.
192. Henry IV. Part firft.
193. Meafure for Meafure.
194. Cato, a Tragedy. By Jofeph Addifon, Efq. 12mo.
195. Euripidis Oreftes, Adjecta eft ad finem verfio Latina ex editione J. Barnes, 8vo.

"Is a very beautiful and correct edition; and it is much to be lamented by the lovers of Greek Literature, that the Univerfity of Glafgow, which hath given the world fuch excellent editions of feveral of the Greek Claffics, and publifhed Æfchylus and Sophocles, had not fufficient encouragement to publifh Euripides in the fame manner."—Harwood, p. 17.

1754.

196. Hiftorical Collections relating to Remarkable Periods of the Succefs of the Gofpel, and Eminent Inftruments employed in promoting it. By John Gillies, D.D. one of the Minifters of Glafgow. 2 vols. 8vo.
197. Pindari quæ fuperfunt omnia, Olympia, Pythia, Nemea, Ifthmia. Gr. 3 vols. fools. 32mo. 2s. 3d.
198. Inftructions of a Father to his Son. To which are added ; a Loving Son's Advice to an Aged Father, and Select Letters on Interefting Subjects. By Sir Walter Rawleigh, 8vo.
199. Young's Satyres, fools. 8vo. fine, 6d., common, 4d.
200. Henry IV. Part Second.

1755.

201. Sommerville's Hobbinol, 8vo. fine, 4d.—12mo. common. 3d.
202. Somerville's Chace, crown 12mo. common, 3d.
203. Moor's Greek Grammar, 8vo.
204. Callimachi Hymni, Gr. writing demy, folio, 5s. fools. folio, 4s.
205. The fame. Writing demy, 4to. 4s. fools. 4to. 2s. 6d.
    " Very correct and beautiful."—Harwood, p. 49.
206. Remarks on Several Parts of Italy, &c. in the years 1701, 2, 3. By the late Right Hon. Jofeph Addifon, Efq. 12mo.
207. The Recruiting Officer, a Comedy. By Mr George Farquhar, 8vo.
208. Fenelon on the Exiftence and Attributes of God. Tranflated from the French by A. Boyer, 8vo. fine paper, 1s. 3d.
209. Ariftophanis Nubes. Gr. ex Editione Kufteri. Latine, ex verfione viri eruditi, Londini, 8vo. 1695, 8vo.
    The large paper copies are in quarto.
210. A Syftem of Moral Philofophy, in three books, written by the late Francis Hutchefon, LL.D Porofeffor of Moral Philofophy in the Univerfity of Glafgow. Publifhed from the Original MS. by his Son, Francis Hutchefon, M.D. With a Memoir of Profeffor Hutchefon, by Principal Leechman. 2 vols. demy 4to. 15s.
211. Selden's Table Talk, fools. 12mo. fine, 9d.

212. Ex Thucydide Inftitutum Funebris Orationis apud Athenienfes; et Periclis Oratio Funebris: Item, Peftis Athenienfis, Gr. et Lat. fools. 12mo. 1s.
213. Leechman's Sermon on the Temper, Character and Duty of a Minifter.
214. Mun on Trade. 8vo. fools. fine, 9d. common crown 12mo. 6d.
215. Edom o' Gordon, 8vo, pp. 12.
> Publifhed by Lord Hailes.—See Percy's Reliques.
216. Young Waters, 8vo.
217. Gill Morice, an Ancient Scots Poem, not before printed, 8vo.
218. Hutchefoni Philofophiæ Moralis Inftitutio Compendiaria. Editio tertia, 8vo.
219. The Works in Profe and Verfe of Dr Thomas Parnell, 8vo.
220. Boileau's Art of Poetry. Tranflated by Sir William Soames, fools. 8vo. pp. 44, fine 4d., common, 3d.

1756.

221. Euclidis Elementa, 4to.
222. The Elements of Euclid, 4to.
> Both these articles were edited by Dr Robert Simson, Professor of Mathematics in the University of Glasgow.
223. Hierocles upon the Golden Verfes of the Pythagoreans. Tranflated immediately out of the Greek into Englifh. With a Preface concerning the Morality of the Heathens in Theory and Practice. Firft Printed in 1682. fools. 8vo. fine 2s., common, 1s. 2d.
224. Logicæ Compendium [by Hutchefon] 12mo.
225. Horatii Opera. Editio tertia, 8vo.
226. Dryden's Poems. 2 vols. 12mo.
227. Homeri Ilias, 2 vols. fools. folio, 17s.
228. Xenophontis Refpublica Lacedæmoniorum. Accedit interpretatio Latina Leunclavii, fools. 8vo. fine, 1s. 2d. common, 9d.
229. An Effay on Difinterefted Love, in a Letter to Bifhop Stillingfleet, by Henry More, D.D. pot 12mo. common, $1\frac{1}{2}$d.
230. The Dublin Society's Weekly Obfervations for the Advancement

of Agriculture and Manufactures, fools. 8vo. fine, 2s. 3d. common paper, 12mo. 1s. 2d.
231. The Flax Huſbandman and Flax Dreſſer Inſtructed : or the beſt Methods of Flax Huſbandry and Flax Dreſſing Explained. In Several Letters, by the Gentleman of the Dublin Society, fools. 8vo. common, 8d.
232. Synopſis Metaphyſicæ. Editio quarta, 8vo.

1757.

233. Theologiæ Chriſtianæ Compendium : Authore Johanne Friderico Oſterwaldio Theologo Neocomenſi. Editio Secunda, crown 12mo. fine, 2s. common, 1s. 6d.
234. Anacreon, Sappho et Alcæus, Gr. 8vo.
   This edition "does great credit to the Univerſity, both in regard to ſplendour and correctneſs."—Harwood, p. 10.
235. Don Quixote. Tranſlated by Motteux, 4 vols. crown 12mo.
236. Gray's Poems, 2 vols.
237. Cicero de Officiis, fools. 8vo. 2s. 6d.
238. Coſmo-Theoros ; or conjectures Concerning the Planetary Worlds and their Inhabitants. Written in Latin by Huygens. Illuſtrated with Plates, fools. 8vo. fine, 1s. 6d., common, 1s. 2d.
239. The Art of Land Meaſuring explained. By John Gray, Teacher of Mathematics in Greenock.
240. Cebetis Tabula. Gr. et Lat. cum notulis, fools. 8vo.

1758.

241. Hamilton of Bangour's Poems. second edition, fools. 8vo. fine, 1s. common, 9d.
242. De Natura Rerum Quæſtiones Philoſophicæ. Authore G. Gordono, 12mo.
243. Young's Love of Fame, 12mo.
244. Epicteti Encheiridion, Gr. et Lat. 8vo.
245. Catalogus Librorum A[rchibaldi] C[ampbell] D[ucis] A[rgatheliæ,] 4to.

246. L'Art Poetique de M. Boileau Defpreaux. fools. 8vo. fine, 3d.
247. Theophrafti Charaƈteres Ethici ex recenfione P. Needham et cum verfione Latina I. Cafauboni, 12mo.
248. P. Virgilii Maronis Opera, ex editione Burmanni, fools. 8vo. fine, 2s. 6d.
> "A very correƈt and beautiful edition."—Harwood, p. 173.

249. Novum Teftamentum ex S. Caftalionis interpretatione. 2 vols. fools. 8vo. fine, 3s. 6d., common, 2s. 3d.
250. The Life and Death of Richard III.
251. Homeri Odyffea, Gr. 2 vols. fools. folio, 17s.—writing demy, folio, 25s.
> This Work completes the edition of Homer's Works in four volumes, folio, referred to at pp. 30, 31. It is "one of the moft fplendid editions of Homer," says Dr Harwood, "ever delivered to the world, and I am informed that its accuracy is equal to its magnificence. Since the publication of the firft edition of this Work, I had occafion carefully to read through this edition, and I did not difcover a single error."—pp. 3, 4.

1759.

252. Titi Lucretii Cari de Rerum Natura Libri Sex, ex editione T. Creech. fools. 8vo. fine, 2s. 6d., common, 1s. 4d.
253. The fame. fools. 4to. 5s.
254. Tyrtæus, fools 4to. 1s. 6d.
255. Thucydides de Bello Peloponnefiaco Libri Oƈto, Gr. et Lat. Ex editione Waffii et Dukeri. 8 vols. fools. 8vo. fine, 17s.
> "I have, at different times, read through this edition of Thucydides four times, and it is by far the moft correƈt of all the Greek Claffics publifhed at Glafgow, and does great credit to that learned Univerfity."—Harwood, p. 25.

256. Davies on the Immortality of the Soul, fools. 8vo. fine, 9d.
257. Effays read to the Literary Society. By James Moor, LL.D. 8vo.
> See Original Papers. No. IV.

258. Tyrtæus' Spartan Leffons. [Tranflated by Dr Moor] 4to.
259. Novum Teftamentum, Græce, fools. 4to. 3s.
260. Julius Cæfar.
261. Henry the Eighth.
262. Logicæ Compendium. Præfixa eft Differtatio de Philofophiæ Origine, ejufque inventoribus aut excultoribus præcipuis, 8vo.

263. Les Œuvres de Boileau, 2 vols. fools. 8vo. fine, 4s.
264. Hoadly on the Terms of Acceptance with God, fools. 8vo. common, 1s. 2d.

1760.

265. Law on Money and Trade. Firſt Printed at Edinburgh, M.D.CC.V. 12mo.
266. Gee on the Trade of Great Britain, fools. 8vo. fine, 1s. 4d. common, 1s.
267. Fenelon's Dialogues on Eloquence in general, and particularly that kind which is fit for the pulpit. Tranſlated by William Stevenſon, M.A. fools. 8vo. fine, 3s. common, 1s. 6d.
268. Fenelon's Fables, compoſed for the uſe of the Duke of Burgundy. Tranſlated by Elphingſton, fools. 8vo. fine, 9d. common, 4d.
269. Horatii Opera. Editio quarta, fools. 8vo. 2s. 6d.
270. The same, fools. 4to. 5s.
271. Motterſhead's Religious Diſcourſes, fools. 8vo. fine, 2s. common, 1s. 2d.
272. Free and Candid Remarks upon the Rev. Mr Motterſhead's Diſcourſe of Baptizing ſick and dying Infants. By the Author of Pædo-Baptiſm. In two Parts. Price Sixpence, 12mo.
273. Coriolanus. By Shakeſpear.
274. Henry V.

1761.

275. The Corruption of this Age and the Remedy thereof, Repreſented in two Letters to a Friend. By the late Rev. Mr Laurence Charteris, &c. pot 12mo. common, 4d.
276. Herodoti Hiſtoria, Gr. et Lat. ex editione Gronovii, 9. vols. fools. 8vo. fine, 21s. pure Greek, fine, 10s. 6d.

"This edition of Herodotus is beautifully printed, and reflects diſtinguiſhed honour on the Univerſity of Glaſgow: I have carefully read it over three times, and have found but few inaccuracies."—Harwood, p. 19.

277. Xenophontis de Socrate Commentarii : item Socratis Apologia, Gr. fools. 4to. 5s.
278. The same, 8vo.

279. The Reverence which is due to the name of God : A Sermon. By William Craig, A.M. one of the Minifters of Glafgow, fools. 8vo. fine, 4d.
280. Milton's Paradife Loft, 2 vols. small 12mo.
281. Anacreon, Sappho, et Alcæus, fools. 32mo., without indexes 9d. with indexes, 1s.
282. An Effay on the Theory of Agriculture, &c. By a Farmer, 12mo.
283. Ciceronis pro Milone oratio ex editione Oliveti, fools. 8vo. common, 4d.
284. Cornelius Nepos.
285. Hudibras, 2 vols. small 12mo.

1762.

286. Synopfis Metaphyficæ. Editio quinta, 8vo.
287. Simfon's Euclid, 8vo.
288. Inftruétions to a Son, &c. By Archibald, Marquis of Argyle, small 12mo.
289. More's Utopia. Tranflated by Burnet, 12mo.
290. Demofthenis Orationes Philippicæ duodecim, Gr. fools. 8vo. fine, 2s. 6d. common, 1s. 6d.
291. Xenophontis Græcorum Res Geftæ et Agefilaus, ex recenfione Walls, Gr. et Lat. 4 vols. 8vo. fine, 7s. 6d. pure Greek, fine, 4s. 8d.
292. Memorials and Letters relating to the Hiftory of Britain in the Reign of James I. [edited by Lord Hailes], 8vo.
293. Direétions to Servants in general, &c. By the Rev. Dr Swift, small fools. 8vo. fine, 6d. common, 3d.
294. Socrates, a Dramatic Poem. By Amyas Bufhe, Esq. A.M. F.R.S. 12mo.
295. His Majefty's Speech to Parliament, 1762, fools. 4to. fine, 2d.
296. Burnet's Paftoral Care, fools. 8vo. common, 1s. 2d.
297. Gray's Fables, 12mo.
298. Ciceronis in Marcum Antonium Orationes prima et fecunda, 8vo. 10d.

1763.

299. Il paftor fido, Tragicommedia Paftorale di Cavalier Guarini, con figure, fools. 8vo. fine, 2s. 6d. common, 1s. 6d.
300. Travels from St Peternfburg in Ruffia to divers parts of Afia. By John Bell of Antermony, 2 vols. 4to.
301. The Republic of Plato. Tranflated from the Greek by Harry Spens, D.D. Minifter of Wemyfs. With a Preliminary Difcourfe concerning the Philofophy of the Ancients by the Tranflator. Writing demy 4to. 9s. fools. 4to. 6s.
302. La Gierufalemme Liberata di Torquato Taffo, 2 vols. fools. 8vo. fine, 5s. common, 3s. 6d.
303. Poems on Several Occafions. By Mr John Philips, Student of Chrift Church, Oxon. To which is added, his Life by Mr George Sewell, fools. 8vo. fine 9d.
304. Paftorals by Mr Ambrofe Philips, fools. 8vo. common, 2d.
305. Longinus de Sublimitate, ex editione tertia Z. Pearce Episcopi Bangorienfis expreffum, Gr. et Lat. 8vo.
306. The same, 4to.
307. M. A. Plauti Comœdiæ, ex editione Gronovii, 3 vols. fools. 8vo. fine, 6s. 6d. common, 2s. 3d.
308. Effay on the End of Tragedy according to Ariftotle. By James Moor, LL.D., 12mo.
309. Difcorfo Sopra le vicende della Letteratura, del Sig. Carlo Denina, fools. 8vo. 2s. 6d.
310. Aminta, Favola Bofcareccia di Torquato Taffo, fools. 8vo. fine, 1s.

1764.

311. A Difcourfe concerning the happinefs of good men and the punifhment of the wicked in the next world. By William Sherlock, D.D., &c. 2 vols. 8vo.
312. Xenophontis Expeditio Cyri. Tomis Quatuor. Ex editione T Hutchefon, Gr. et Lat. fools. 8vo.
313. Hutchefon's Compend of Moral Philofophy, third edition, 2 vols. 8vo.

314. Clarendon's Effays, 12mo.
315. Logicæ Compendium. Editio quinta, 8vo.
316. Meditations of Antoninus, 2 vols. 12mo.
317. Hiftory of the Feuds and Conflicts among the Clans, &c. fools. 8vo. common, 9d.

1765.

318. The Works of the ever memorable John Hales of Eton. Edited by Lord Hailes, 3 vols. 12mo.
319. A Prefent for an Apprentice : or a Sure Guide to gain both Efteem and Eftate. With Rules for his conduct to his Mafter, and in the World, &c. By a late Lord Mayor of London, crown 12mo. 3d.
320. A Catalogue of the Books which remain unfold of the Library of the late Mr. Robert Dick, Profeffor of Natural Philofophy in the Univerfity of Glafgow, which begins to be fold by auction at R. and A. Foulis's Auction-Room in the Old Coffee Houfe, on Monday the 18th of February, 1765, at 6 o'clock at night. Commiffions directed to R. and A. Foulis will be carefully obferv'd, 12mo.

> Note at the end of this Catalogue,—"In two or three days will be publifhed, a Catalogue of the Large and Valuable Library of the Rev. Mr Alexander Campbell, late Minifter of the Gofpel at Inverara."

321. Lactantius' Relation of the Death of the Primitive Perfecutors, Englifhed by Gilbert Burnett, D.D. To which is prefixed, a Difcourfe concerning Perfecution, demy 18mo. fine, 9d. common, 4d.
322. Cato, a Tragedy. By Jofeph Addifon, Esq., small 12mo.
323. Milton's Minor Poems, 12mo.
324. Le Siege de Calais, Tragedie. Par M. de Belloy, fools. 8vo. fine, 9d. common, 6d.
325. Milton's Paradife Regained, 12mo.
   The following Plays by Shakefpeare :—
326. The Life and Death of King John.
327. The Taming of a Shrew.
328. All's well that ends well.
329. Twelfth Night.

330. Winter's Tale.
331. Richard II.
332. Henry VI., Parts Firft, Second, and Third.
333. Timon of Athens.
334. Antony and Cleopatra.
335. Titus Andronicus.
336. Troilus and Creffida.
337. Cymbeline.
338. Romeo and Juliet.
339. Comedy of Errors.
340. Much Ado about Nothing.
341. As you Like it.
342. Georgii Buchanani Paraphrafis Pfalmorum Davidis Poetica, fools. 8vo. fine, 2s. 6d.

1766.

343. Milton's Paradife Loft, 2 vols. 12mo.
344. Memorials and Letters Relating to the Hiftory of Britain in the Reign of James I. Publifhed from the originals. Second Edition Corrected and Enlarged, 8vo.
345. Memorials and Letters Relating to the Hiftory of Britain in the Reign of Charles I., 8vo.
346. The Manuel of Epictetus, 12mo.
347. Somerville's Poems, 12mo.
348. Catalogue of Books to be Sold by Auction by R. and A. Foulis, 4to.
349. Confeffion of Faith, 8vo.
350. Moor on the Prepofitions of the Greek Language, writing demy, 8vo. 9d.
351. Vindication of Virgil from the charge of puerility imputed to him by Dr Pearce, 12mo. pp. 32. [by Dr James Moor] writing demy, 8vo. 9d. fools. 8vo. 4½d.
352. Moor's Greek Grammar, second edition.
353. Ramfay on Education, fools. 8vo. fine, 3d., common, 2½d.
354. An Account of the Prefervation of King Charles II. after the Battle of Worcefter, drawn up by himfelf; to which is added his

Letters to Several Perfons, with a Preface and Notes, [by Lord Hailes] writing demy, 8vo. 1s. 6d.
355. Shakefpear, 8 vols. crown 12mo. common 12s.
356. The fame, 16 vols. fools. 8vo. fine, 24s.
See page 23.

1767.

357. Chriftian Unity Illuftrated and Recommended from the Example of the Primitive Church. A Sermon Preached before the Synod of Glafgow and Ayr, at Glafgow, October 14, 1766. By William Dalrymple, A.M. one of the Minifters of Ayr, fools. 8vo. fine, 4d.
358. An Effay on the Life of Jefus Chrift. By William Craig, D.D. one of the Minifters of Glafgow, writing demy, 8vo. 1s. 8d., fools. 8vo. 1s. 2d..
359. Compend of Phyfics, 8vo.
360. Telemachus, a Mafk, 12mo.
361. Parnell's Works in Profe and Verfe, 12mo.
362. The Marquis of Worcefter's Scantlings of Inventions, fools. 12mo. 9d.
363. Pope's Homer, 7 vols. small 12mo.
364. Xenophontis Cyropædia, Gr. et Lat. 4 vols. fools. 8vo. fine, 7s. 6d., common, 3s.
365. Effay on Religion and Morality, 8vo.

1768.

366. Pope's Homer's Odyffey, 3 vols. 18mo.
367. Pope's Poems, 4 vols. 18mo.
368. Drummond's Polemo-Middinia, fools. 4to. 3d.
369. The Modern Farmer's Guide, 2 vols. 8vo.
370. An Account of Corfica, the Journal of a Tour to that Ifland, and Memoirs of General Paoli. By James Bofwell, Efq. 8vo.
371. Gray's Poems, [edited by Dr Beattie] 4to. medium paper, 3s. 6d.
372. Ramfay's Tea Table Mifcellany, 2 vols. fools. 8vo. fine, 3s. common, 1s. 6d.

1769.

373. Dryden's Virgil, 3 vols. 18mo.
374. Catalogue containing a valuable Collection of Books, confifting chiefly of two Libraries lately purchased : which will begin to be fold by auction at the Old Coffee Houfe on Wednefday next, the 11th of January, 1769. The time of the fale from fix o'clock at night to nine, 4to.
375. Catalogue of Books to be Sold by Auction by R. & A. Foulis, 4to.
376. Poems on Several Occafions. By Matthew Prior, Efq. 2 vols. fools. 18mo. 2s.
377. Hutchefon on the Nature and Conduct of the Paffions, fools. 8vo.
378. Ciceronis pro Marcello et Ligario Orationes, ex editione Oliveti, 8vo. fine, 6d., common 4d.
379. Leechman's Sermon on the Temper, Character, and Duty of a Minifter of the Gofpel, seventh edition, 12mo.
380. Leechman's Sermon on Prayer, sixth edition, 12mo.
381. Young's Night Thoughts, 2 vols. 18mo.

1770.

382. Vindication of the Sacred Books from the mifreprefentations and cavils of M. de Voltaire. By Dr Findlay, one of the Minifters of Glafgow, demy 8vo. 4s.
383. Anacreon, Sappho, et Alcæus. Gr. et Lat. fools. 8vo. fine, 1s. 2d.
384. Memorables of the Montgomeries, fools. 4to. fine 3d. common, 2d.
385. Milton's Paradife Loft, writing demy, folio, 17s. fools. folio, 10s. 6d.
386. Compend of Phyfics, 12mo.
387. Moor's Greek Grammar, 8vo.
388. Stonehoufe's Spiritual Directions, fools. 8vo. fine, 4d. common, 3d.
389. Pindari Opera, Gr. et Lat. 2 vols. fools. 8vo. fine, 3s 6d. common, 2s.
390. The Gallery of Raphael, folio.
391. Dryden's Poems, 2 vols. 12mo.
392. Gray's Poems, 18mo.
393. Inftructions for Officers, with Plates, 8vo.

394. The Life of God in the Soul of Man, &c. By Henry Scougal, late Profeffor of Divinity in the Univerfity of Aberdeen. With a Preface by Bifhop Burnet. And Rules and Inftructions for a Holy Life, by Archbifhop Leighton, fools. 12mo. fine, 9d., common, 4d.

1771.

395. Cebetis Tabula, Gr. et Lat.
396. Don Quixote. Tranflated by Motteux. 4 vols. crown 12mo. fine, 6s., middle, 3s. 6d., common, 3s. 6d.
397. Pope's Homer, 4 vols. 18mo.
398. Confiderations upon a Bankrupt Law for Scotland, 4to.
399. Collins' and Hammond's Poems, 18mo.
400. Denham's Poems, 18mo.
402. Tentamen Medicum Inaugurale de Angina Maligna. Auctore Joanne Storer, 8vo.

1772.

402. Filli di Sciro, Favola Paftorale del C. Guidobaldo de Bonarelli con le figure di Sebaftiano le Clerc. Primieramente Stampata in Ferrara MDCVII. fools, 8vo. fine, 1s. 6d. common, 1s. 2d.
403. Ciceronis Orationes.
404. Hutchefon's Enquiry into the Original of our Ideas of Beauty and Virtue, &c. fools. 8vo. fine, 2s. 3d. common, 1s. 2d.
405. Hutchefon's Compend of Moral Philofophy. Fourth edition, 12mo.
406. Logicæ Compendium, 12mo.
407. Letters concerning the true foundation of Virtue or Moral Goodnefs, wrote in a correfpondence between Mr Gilbert Burnet and Mr Francis Hutchefon, fools. 8vo. fine, 1s. 2d. common, 9d.
408. Hutchefon's Effay on the Nature and Conduct of the Paffions. Third edition, fools. 8vo. fine, 2s. 6d. common, 1s. 2d.
409. Beggar's Opera, 12mo.

1773.

410. Gray and Littleton's Poems, 18mo.

411. Smollet's Ode to Independence, [publiſhed by Profeſſor Richard-ſon], 4to.
 "A few copies only of this poem were thrown off at Glaſgow."—*Edin. Mag.* I. 25.
412. Reports to the Lords Commiſſioners of Police, relative to the Navigation of the Rivers Forth, Gudie, and Devon. M.DCC.LXXIII. [By the celebrated James Watt], 4to. with a large Map.
413. Parnell's Poems, fools. 8vo. fine, 1s. 4d.
414. Moor's Greek Grammar, 8vo.
415. Poems by Thomas Graham, 12mo.
416. The Meditations of Saint Auguſtine, His Treatiſe of the Love of God, Soliloquies, and Manuel. Tranſlated by George Stanhope, D.D. &c., fools. 8vo. fine 2s. common, 1s. 2d.
417. The Seven Cartoons of Raphael. By W. Mitchell and W. Buchanan, folio.
418. Diſſertatio Inauguralis de Hyſteria, Auctore Samuele Evans, 8vo.

1774.

419. Liberty, a Poem. By James Thomſon, 18mo.
420. Poems, chiefly Rural. [By William Richardſon, Eſq. Profeſſor of Humanity in the Univerſity of Glaſgow], 8vo.
421. Of the Imitation of Jeſus Chriſt. In Four Books. By Thomas à Kempis, fools. 8vo. fine, 1s. 6d. common, 1s.
422. Burrow's Book of Rates, folio.
423. Metaphyſicæ Synopſis, editio ſexta, 8vo. pp. 151.
424. Swift's Poems, 4 vols. 18mo.

1775.

425. Select Poems from a larger Collection, 18mo.
426. Euripidis Medea, Gr. et Lat., fools. 8vo. fine, 1s. 2d. common, 9d.
427. The same, fools. 4to. fine, 2s. 6d.
428. Dryden's Virgil, 3 vols. 18mo.
429. Epicteti Enchiridion, Gr. et Lat. ex editione J. Upton.
430. Jepthes ſive Votum, Tragœdia. Auctore Georgio Buchanano, Scoto, fools. 8vo. fine, 4d. common, 3d.

431. The Funeral Oration of Lewis XV. the Well-beloved, King of France and Navarre. Pronounced in the Church of the Royal Abbey of St Denis, the 27 of July, 1774. By Meffire de Beauvais, Lord-Bifhop of Senez, fools. 8vo. fine, 8d. common, 4d.
432. Sherlock on Death, fools. 8vo. fine, 2s. common, 1s. 2d.
433. Garth's Poems, 18mo.
434. Richardfon's Epithalamium on the Marriages of the Dutchefs of Athol and the Honourable Mrs Graham, 4to.
435. Poems, chiefly Rural. Third edition corrected, 12mo.

1776.

436. Simfoni Opera quædam reliqua, Sciz. Apollonii Pergæi de Sectione determinata Libri II. reftituti, duobus infuper libris aucti : porifmatum liber : de logarithmis liber : de limitibus quantitatum et rationum fragmentum : et appendix, pauca continens problemata ad illuftrandam præcipue veterum geometrarum analyfin : edita impenfis quidem Philippi Comitis de Stanhope, curâ vero Jacobi Clow, Phil. Prof. Glafg., 4to.
437. Select Sermons on Interefting Subjects. By Hugh Knox, D.D. &c. 2 vols. 12mo.
438. Hamlet, Prince of Denmark, 12mo.
439. Gay's Poems, and Beggar's Opera, 2 vols. 12mo.
440. Denham's Poems, 12mo.
441. A Catalogue of Pictures, compofed and painted chiefly by the moft admired Mafters of the Roman, Florentine, Parman, Bolognefe, Venetian, Flemifh, and French Schools. In which many of the moft capital are illuftrated by Defcriptions and Critical Remarks. Humbly offered to the Impartial Examination of the Public, by Robert Foulis. In Three Volumes. London, Sold at the place of exhibition, 12mo.

<small>There can be no doubt that this Catalogue was printed at Glasgow. The following entry appears in the List of Debts owing by the deceased Robert & Andrew Foulis,—" Sum due to the defuncts for outlaid expenfe of Catalogue of Paintings, £42. 2. 9."</small>

LIST OF BOOKS,

THE DATES OF WHICH HAVE NOT BEEN ASCERTAINED.

442. Hutchesoni Oratio Inauguralis, fools. 8vo. 9d.
443. Tully on Friendship, fools. 8vo. fine, 4d. common, 3d.
444. The Devil on Two Sticks, pot 12mo. common, 9d.
445. Christ's Kirk on the Green, fools. 8vo. fine, 3d. common, 2½d.
446. Milton's Samson Agonistes, pot 12mo. common, 2d.
447. Milton's Tractate on Education, fools. 12mo. ½d.
448. The Freeholder's Political Catechism, fools. 8vo. fine, 2½d. common, 2d.
449. M'Gill's Synod Sermon, fools. 8vo. fine, 4d.
450. Cappe's Sermon, fools. 8vo. fine, 3d. common, 2d.
451. Du Fresnoy's Judgment of Painters, fools. 8vo. 3d.
452. Coypel Sur la Peinture, fools. 8vo. fine, 2½d.
453. Ramsay on the Love of God, fools. 8vo. fine 3d. common, 2d.
454. Voltaire's Charles XII., fools. 8vo. common, 1s.
455. The Abridgement or Summarie of the Scots Chronicle. By John Monipennie. First printed at Britaines Bursse by John Budge, 1612. [With a map, no date], fools. 8vo. fine, 9d. common, 4½d.
456. La destruction des Jesuites, fools. 8vo. fine, 1s.
457. Prince Eugene and King Henry's Prayer, fools. 8vo. fine, 3d.
458. Bishop Taylor's Rules for the Clergy, fools. 8vo. 4d.
459. Milton's l'Allegro and Il Penseroso, fools. 4to. 3d.
460. Doctor Wight's Heads of Lectures, fools. 8vo. fine, 6d. common, 4d. With the Chronological Table, 6d.
461. Dalrymple's Address to the Americans, fools. 8vo. fine, 6d. common, 3d.
462. American Querist, fools. 8vo. fine, 4d. common, 2d.
463. Plain Reasons for being a Christian, crown 8vo. 2d.

464. Shaftefbury's Moralift, crown 12mo. 1s.
465. Shaftefbury's Characteriftics.
466. Hiero on the Condition of a Tyrant, fools. 8vo. 3d.
467. Bennet on the Cruelty of the Church of Rome, fools. 8vo.
468. Sermon on Early Piety, 8vo.
469. Reprefentation for the Brewers in Glafgow.
470. Fannuel's Funeral Oration, fools. 4to.
471. Cudworth's Sermon, 8vo.
472. Fenelon's Pious Thoughts, fools. 8vo. fine, 1s. 2d. common, 9d.

The following English Poets in pot 12mo.

473. Dryden's Fables, 2 vols.
474. Waller's Poems.
475. Young's Love of Fame the Univerfal Paffion, and other Poems.
476. Thomfon's Seafons.
477. Thomfon's Caftle of Indolence, and other Poems.
478. Mafon's Poems, 2 vols.
479. Glover's Leonidas.
480. Shenftone's Select Poems.
481. Aikenfide's Pleafures of Imagination.
482. Parnell's Poems.
483. Swift's Select Poems, 2 vols.
484. Modern Poems.
485. Orphan.
486. Rofamond, by Addifon.
487. The Drummer : or the Haunted Houfe, by the same.
488. Fair Penitent, by Rowe.
489. Lady Jane Gray, by the same.
490. Jane Shore, by the same.
491. Ramfay's Scots Proverbs.
492. Cebes [in English].
493. Chevy Chace, according to the Scots and Englifh editions, 4to.
494. Tucker on Naturalization.
495. Archimedes, Gr. folio.
496. Butler's Sermons.

497. Butler's Analogy, 2 vols.
498. Scougal's Sermons.
499. Macbeth.
500. Othello.
501. Hamlet.
502. Hardyknute, a Fragment of an Antient Scots Poem, 4to. Price Sixpence, [1745].
503. Propofals for Encouraging by Subfcription an Academy for Painting and Sculpture at Glafgow, [cir. 1758].
504. Leechman on Prayer, 8vo. [1749].
505. Poems on Several Occafions. By the Rev. Mr John Pomfret. Twelfth edition, 8vo. [1757].
506. La Pucelle d'Orleans, Poeme Heroi-Comique, 18mo. *Chez les Frères Follis*, [1756].
507. Vertot's Revolutions of Portugal, fools 8vo. fine, 1s. 2d. common, 8d. [1758].
508. A Difcourfe on Ancient and Modern Learning. By the late Right Hon. Jofeph Addifon, Efq. Fourth edition, fools. 8vo. fine, 3d. common, 2d. [1759].
509. Epicteti Enchiridion ex editione J. Upton, 64mo. [1765].
510. Addifon's Poems, fools. 8vo. [1770].
511. A Catalogue of Books, lately imported from France, containing the fcarceft and moft elegant editions of the Greek and Roman authors, printed by the Aldi, Juntæ, the Stephens, Turnebus, Vafcofan, the Morells, &c. [cir. 1744].
512. Books Printed by Robert and Andrew Foulis, Printers to the Univerfity of Glafgow. The Prices of the Books, in quires or fewed in blue paper, are affixed, 8vo. pp. 51. [cir. 1775].
513. A Catalogue of Pictures, Drawings, Prints, Statues, and Bufts in Plaifter of Paris, done at the Academy in the Univerfity. In this Catalogue is inferted a Collection of Prints, the Plates of which are the property of R. and A. Foulis. Publifhed for the ufe of Subfcribers, folio. [Reprinted in this volume, from a copy in the poffession of David Laing, Esq.]

514. A Catalogue of Books, being the entire Stock in Quires, of the late Meffieurs Robert and Andrew Foulis, Printers to the Univerfity of Glafgow : confifting of their elegant and correct editions of the Greek and Latin Claffics, and other books printed by them; and likewife of the Books in Quires printed by Others which were in their poffeffion; Intended to be Sold in Wholefale by Private Bargain, &c.—Glasgow, October 1st, 1777, 4to.

Though neither this, nor the two following articles were printed by R. and A. Foulis, they are inserted as relating to them.

515. A Catalogue of a Large Collection of Copper-Plates, [cir. 1777].
516. A Catalogue of Paintings, and of Moulds for cafting Bufts, Statues, &c. in Plaifter of Paris, [cir. 1777].

NOTICES

REGARDING THE

ACADEMY ESTABLISHED AT GLASGOW,

BY

ROBERT AND ANDREW FOULIS.

NOTICES

REGARDING THE

ACADEMY ESTABLISHED AT GLASGOW,

BY

ROBERT AND ANDREW FOULIS.

THE origin, and a few subsequent facts in the history of this institution have already been noticed in an earlier part of the work, but as a minute account of it would have confused the narrative, and as the documents regarding the Academy form by much the largest part of those which remain, a more detailed notice of it may not be unacceptable.

The History of the Fine Arts in Scotland does not seem to have attracted much notice till of late years, when the study of every thing connected with the History, Literature, and Antiquities of the country has become fashionable. A paper, containing some curious facts on this subject, appeared in "The Bee," vol. xviii. p. 76, and is believed to have been written by Sir G. Chalmers. In 1799, when the late Mr. Pinkerton published his "Scottish Gallery," he prefixed an "Introduction on the Rise and Progress of Painting in Scotland," in which he has collected many interesting notices of the Scotch artists. The only painter referred to by him of whom much is known, is George Jameson, the pupil of Rubens, and fellow-student of Vandyke, who attracted the notice of Charles I. while in Scotland in 1633, and to whom that monarch sat for his portrait.* The names of the other Scotch artists,— the elder and younger Scougal, Paton, Aikman, Alexander, and Medina, are now little known except to collectors. No traces have been discovered of the practice of the Fine Arts in Glasgow beyond the visits of some itinerant " Dick Tinto," and the portraits of a few of the benefactors to the city which adorn the interior of some of our public buildings. One notice, connected with this subject, appears in the very curious collections of extracts from the Burgh Records, which have been lately printed in the Glasgow Courier, by William Motherwell, Esq., and it deserves notice, as showing the remuneration which labour of this kind received :—" 12th June, 1641. The faid day ordanis the threafaurer to have ane warrand to pay to James Colquhoun fyve dollars for drawing of the portraiƈt of the toun to be fent to Holland." It has been suggested that this " portraiƈt " was probably intended for Bleau's Atlas, which was preparing for publication at Amsterdam about this time, although it did not appear till 1654.

To proceed in our account of the Glasgow Academy.—It will be readily believed that Foulis's motives for establishing that institution must have had their rise purely in his own ardent attachment to the Fine Arts. The field which Scotland then afforded for such an undertaking was extremely limited, and the country was at that time only recovering from the effects of the recent rebellion. But Foulis probably felt confident that were such an institution once established, its ultimate

---

* " When the king was at Edinburgh, 1633, the magistrates procured from Jameson many of his portraits, with which they adorned the sides of the Netherbow." (Pinkerton's Introd.) It is perhaps to some of his productions that Spalding alludes in his very quaint and amusing account of his majesty's entrance into the city :—" At the weft end of the tolbuith he [the king] faw the royall pedegree of the kings of Scotland, frae Fergus the Firft, delecately painted ; and ther had ane fourth fpeech," &c. (Spalding's History of the Troubles. Bannatyne Club Edit. v. i. p. 16). An equally amusing notice on the same subject occurs in Craufurd's History of the University of Edinburgh, p. 120. Other notices of George Jameson, burgess of " glorious Aberdeen," occur in Spalding's work. He was probably the same person, as Jameson the artist is stated by Pinkerton to have been an Aberdonian.

success might be considered as almost certain,—and that those who should acquire a taste for the Arts might "infpire the fame love and relifh for the beautiful in thofe that are near them, and they in others." The very fact that there was then no other Academy for the Arts in Scotland seems to have operated powerfully in inducing him to commence the undertaking. The field was entirely unoccupied, and those who were willing to encourage the rising institutions of their country could not plead the number or variety of those which required their patronage as an excuse for withholding their assistance from it. He had, besides, hopes of meeting even with royal patronage,—hopes which were soon blasted by the untimely death of the Prince of Wales.*

Two plans seem to have been proposed for the support of the Academy. The first was, to submit the scheme to some person of high rank; but this idea was, after mature consideration, abandoned. The second, to use Foulis's own words, was to communicate it to some merchants of spirit, and represent it to them as a finer kind of manufacture, that would take a longer time to come to a bearing and produce profit, but that in the end would make full amends for the delay, by affording more ample profits, because the manufactures were not produced from dear materials, and the productions were considered not so much according to the quantity of labour they contained, as according to the degree of genius and art well conducted. This plan seems to have been adopted, but nothing farther is known of the Academy till 1759, when the following "Propofal for encouraging by Subfcription an Academy for Painting and Sculpture," was inserted in the Scots Magazine. It appears to have been issued the year before.

" Propofal.—The productions of Mr Foulis' Academy being expofed to view at Edinburgh in the Shop of Mr Robert Fleming, and at Glafgow in the Gallery appointed for them in the College; It is propofed, That fuch gentlemen as are willing to promote this defign, fhall advance cer-

---

* Preface to Foulis's Catalogue of Pictures.

tain fums annually, for any number of years they fhall think proper; during which time they are to chufe, among the Prints, Defigns, Paintings, Models, or Cafts, which are the production of this Academy, fuch lots as may amount to the value of the fums they have advanced. The Subfcribers fhall have a receipt for the fums refpectively paid by them, figned either by Mr Foulis at Glafgow, or Mr Fleming, his Truftee, at Edinburgh. Gentlemen may withdraw their fubfcriptions when they pleafe."*

It appears from a letter prefixed to this Proposal, that Foulis had already experienced much difficulty in the selection of proper teachers, and that he had to contend with the predilection of the nation for the works of foreign artists; so much so, that although the productions of the Academy had now become numerous, he found it no easy matter to dispose of them to any advantage. He had now several students, some of whom had made considerable progress. While employed at Glasgow, they seem to have received such wages as they might have got had they followed a mechanical employment,—and if they exhibited sufficient marks of genius, they were sent abroad to study at the expense of the Academy. The first of those who went abroad in this manner was a young man of the name of Maxwell, who died soon after his arrival at Rome. The second was William Cochrane, of whose life a short sketch will be afterwards given, and the last was Archibald Maclauchlane,† who was subsequently married to one of Robert Foulis's daughters.‡

Of the transactions at the Academy we have but little information. The following extracts from letters, written at different periods, contain almost all that is known. The first was written in 1753 or 1754.

---

* Scots Mag. 1759, p. 47.

† One of the best copies by Maclauchlane, while at Rome, was from Raphael's celebrated picture of the School of Athens. "This work," says Lord Buchan, "fell into the hands of a dealer, where it was much injured, and afterwards, through neglect, almoft quite deftroyed." (Some Memoranda concerning the Undertaking of Messrs Foulis, Printers at Glasgow, p. 9, note).

‡ Mrs Dewar to the Earl of Buchan, May, 1808. Richardson's Letter, p. 12.

"The Magazines of Vertù have not yet efcaped the dangers of the feas, but thofe that have arrived anfwer the expectations of the public, fo as to excite an univerfal curiofity. The Saint Cecilia fupports his character as an original of Raphael, and the Carrying to the Tomb, an original by the fame mafter, is one of the nobleft pieces of painting I ever faw. The Duke of Hamilton having generoufly offered us the liberty of copying or engraving an[y] of his pictures, the painter is ftill there. He finifhed firft a copy of the Supper of Emmaus by Titian, and his copy is efteemed a faithful and beautiful reprefentation of the original. The next picture he attempted was the moft celebrated picture in Scotland,—Daniel in the Den of Lions,*—the fize of life, an original picture by Rubens, for which it is faid the family refufed a thoufand guineas. This picture, by reafon of its great dimenfions, cou'd not be copy'd without making a thoro' trial of the abilities of the copyift, which oblig'd him to copy at a great diftance from the original, and this is fo well approv'd, that I have not heard one that have [has] feen it, that has not declared great fatiffaction. It was finifh'd a few days ago, and placed up in the Duke['s] gallery on his birthday. I have been affured by feveral that were prefent, that it gave univerfal fatiffaction to a great company of nobility and gentry who were prefent. He has now begun to copy a picture of a Treaty between England and Germany or Flanders in queen Elizabeth's time. This picture is not only valuable as a piece of painting, but as a piece of hiftory, and [for] the portraits of fo many celebrated perfons, all whofe names are on the picture. It belonged to the Earl of Sunderland, and was made a prefent of by him to the then Earl of Hamilton. The ftory is, that my Lord Sunderland gave him the choice of all his pictures; not expecting that he wou'd have chofen that one, he offered him his choice of any other two to part with it. The next we propofe to copy in Hamilton

---

* "Glafcuæ Octob. 1767. Jacobus Coutts Efq[r.] Mebr. Parliamenti pro urbe Edinburgo, ac eminens *Banker* Londini, vifitabat Academiam hic, ac emit a Rob. et And. Foulis picturas fupra valorem £100 Sterl. inter quas emit picturam Danielis in fpecu Leonum, magnæ formæ pret. 50 Guineas." Fleming's Diary.

is a portrait of the Earl of Danby by Vandyke; but before that is done, I am determined to have him return to Glafgow to work after nature and Raphael, and in the beginning of winter to expofe all that is hitherto done to public view, in order to excite emulation, and to have fome little prizes for drawing. We have one scholar already, from whom we expect reputation and good fervice. Our engraver is employ'd in doing a full-length picture of the Duke of Argyle; as it is large,—all done with the graver,—and a great deal of work in feveral parts of it, I don't expect to fee it publifhed before winter. If its appearance on paper be fuitable to its appearance on copper, it will be a mafterpeice."

The next letter relative to the Academy is dated January, 1763, and addressed by Robert Foulis to Mr Yorke. William Cochrane, the artist, who is mentioned in it, after having given sufficient proofs of his genius at Glasgow, was sent to the continent, where he remained for five years,*—principally at Rome, and under the celebrated Gavin Hamilton. "I am greatly obliged to you," says Robert Foulis, "for the kind manner in which you received Willy Cochrane, for the recommendations you honoured him with, and above all for your procuring for him a fafe paffage in a man-of-war, where he met with the greateft civilities and kindnefs on your account, and arrived at Naples free from [of] all expence. I am perfuaded, at his return, he will be a hiftory painter of a rank to do honour to his benefactors and his country.

"The Academy is now coming into a ftate of tolerable maturity. We have modelling, engraving, original hiftory-painting, and portrait painting,—all in a reputable degree of perfection. In the morning our more advanced ftudents sketch hiftorical fubjects from Plutarch's Lives and other ancient books. The day is employed in painting and engraving, and by the younger fcholars in drawing. In the evening they draw three days a week after a model, and other three after cafts of plaifter from the antique."

Cochrane ultimately returned to Glasgow, where he practised as a

---

* Mrs Dewar to the Earl of Buchan, May, 1808.

portrait painter for many years. Attachment to an aged mother induced him to remain there, and consequently he never rofe to that eminence which he might otherwise have attained. He died in October, 1785, at the early age of forty-seven, and by permission of the magistrates a marble tablet was erected to his memory in the choir of the cathedral.*

An imperfect letter, addressed to a nobleman in February, 1764, gives the following account of the labours of the students :—

"We have lately caft off a few fetts of the principal prints we have engrav'd : They wou'd make a volume between 60 and 70 fheets of royal paper the full breadth of the fheet. Charles Cordiner has made three drawings, 2 after the ruins of the Caftle of Bothwell, and one after the Caftle of Crookfton, with the Ewe Tree, which I have caufed to be neatly etched, and put his name to them as ye drawer. He is now able to make a good copy of any picture, and I propofe to try him foon at portraits. We are fucceeding pretty well in that branch. The portrait of my Lord and Lady Glencairn, the two young ladies, Lady Dorothy Primrofe, and other wch we have done, among which are feveral full-lengths, have been generally commended."

Nothing is known of the progress of the academicians at a later date, except what Foulis himself has said in the preface to the catalogue of pictures in 1776.

"The Effays in Landfcape that were done by Robert Paul a little before his death have that fimplicity which promifes fuperior excellence. His view of the weft ftreet, called the Trongate, of Glafgow, is the moft capital, as it is the laft of his works, and was finifhed after his death by William Buchanan.

"There are a confiderable number of the prints in Raphael's Bible done by the late William Buchanan which fhow his ability as a drawer and engraver. His Paul preaching at Athens and the other Cartoons he engraved, and laft of all, Raphael's Tranffiguration, which he had

---

* Life of Cochrane in Chalmers' Biograph. Dict.   His epitaph is inserted in Scots Mag.. 1810, p. 97.

nearly finifhed when he died, done from the picture reverfed in a mirror, are convincing proofs of his merit.

"Nor can I neglect on this occafion to do juftice to James Mitchell, who, although the nearnefs of his fight difqualified him for a common profeffion, yet in a few weeks made a furprizing progrefs, and his engravings, after he attained experience, have been favourably received by the public. Several of his performances in Raphael's Bible are much fuperior, both in conception and execution, to Chaperon. His print of Daniel in the Den of Lions, after Rubens' picture in his Grace the Duke of Hamilton's Collection, has been well received. He engraved alfo four of the Cartoons, Mount Parnaffus and the School of Athens, and has laboured with fuccefs both after Raphael and Correggio.

"The Effays in original Hiftory-Painting that have been finifhed are not numerous; but there are fome which were done at Rome by Meffieurs Cochrane and M'Lauchlane that do them honor, although their manners are fo different that their works cannot be compared with propriety.

"There are fome drawings and pictures by David Allan, before he went abroad, that are done with invention and fpirit, and are furprizing at fo early a period."

The last letter on this subject which we shall insert, was written by Robert Foulis to Lord Mountstuart in 1776.

"Robert Foulis, Printer to the Univerfity of Glafgow, prefents his humble refpects to Lord Mount-Stuart to acquaint his Lordfhip, that he prefumes to give him this trouble, encouraged by Colonel Edmonfton, by Mr Thomas Kennedy his nephew, and by Mr Campbell of Shawfield. The circumftance of the death of his brother and other friends, and his own advancement to the extremity of life having made it proper that he fhould put an end to his labours in the fervice of the Fine Arts, and difpofe of his Collections; in that view he has brought to London his Prints, Drawings, and Pictures. Three nights' Sale of the Prints are in a Catalogue that comes along with this: the whole would have been continued, but Mr Sandford's engagements permitted no more, and he was of opinion that it was too many for the intereft of the Proprietor, as it was fo late in the year. His Collection, which will likewife be difpofed off, of Drawings is very numerous, and contains capital defigns of the leading mafters and their difciples of every fchool. He printed a Catalogue of his Pictures before he left Glafgow, containing defcriptions and critical remarks, which were made when in view of the Pictures, one of which he has fent by the Bearer, which he hopes Lord Mount Stuart will be fo good as to accept. He will find the Collection made in Syftem, and as the Collector believed the Roman School enjoyed more advantages than any other, and Raphael the greateft mafter and moft amiable genius that ever any of the fchools poffeffed, fo he accordingly directed his ambition to acquire as many pictures and drawings of Raphael as he could poffibly difcover by the moft diligent fearch. What fuccefs he had has appeared to thofe who have been able and willing to examine the pictures; the whole makes a progrefs of Raphael from his early times to his laft period, and on that account are curious, as they fhow his gradual progrefs and changes of manner; but there are five or fix fo capital, that I have never heard of any Collection on fale, that contained fo many. Neither his pictures in the Vatican, nor thofe procured by princes, nor thofe fixed in public places have ever entered into commerce, which renders it difficult to procure capital pictures of this Mafter, yet in this Collection will be found, upon a ftrict examination, an original of the Carrying of our Saviour to the Tomb, more perfect than the Borghefe,—an original of the Saint Cecilia on a different ground from the Bologna, the one being a landfcape with a blue fky, and the other completely dark without landfcape, and the figures much improved, particularly in expreffion. Alfo a picture of Theagenes and Chariclea in the Temple of Diana, of wonderful grace, and of which I have never heard of any repetition; the Refurrection of our Saviour, of which the firft effay, which is not fo compleat in grouping or expreffion, has been engraved. But there is one picture more, the Tranffiguration, not fo large as the Roman picture, but in many other refpects better; your Lordfhip will find the differences in the Catalogue, and the grounds of its priority, which has been proved to the fatiffaction of painters, and many excellent judges, and is ftill fubmitted to the reviews of all who choofe to examine. I forefee from the prefent unfavorable circumftances, that these pictures will be tranfported to fome foreign country, whereas were they joyned to the Cartoons, they would be found to have merit equal to theirs, and to be preferable as finifhed pictures before patterns for tapeftry. Forgive this trouble from one who has been long honoured with the patronage of Lord Bute, although diftance and other circumftances have made him in a manner forgot."

Although the Academy has always, and deservedly, been considered a failure, it was the means of raising David Allan and James Tassie from obscurity. In regard to the last of these, it deserves particularly to be noticed, that his first relish for the Fine Arts arose from visiting the Academy on a holiday, when the pictures were exposed gratis to public view.* It has not been considered necessary to give any outline of the lives of these persons, as their history is already well known.

The Catalogue of Pictures, &c. to which this prefixed, and for the use of which the writer is indebted to the kindness of David Laing, Esq. is without date. The "Jerusalem Delivered" and "Aminta" of Tasso are mentioned in it as intended for publication, illustrated with Le Clerc's designs. These, and several other Italian works in the same form, were printed in 1763, and this may in some measure fix the date. It will show better than any description that could be given, the extent to which the labours of the artists at Glasgow were carried.

---

* One of these occasions is thus noticed in the Diary of Mr John Fleming, "à Glafgow 4. Juin, 1770. Anjourd'hui, Lundi, fut célébré la naiffance du Roi. Les Tableaux appartenans à Meffrs. Foulis dans l'Academie à Glafgow etoient exhibées dans la Cour interieure de l'Académie ici. Il y avoit la foule grande pour les regarder."

A CATALOGUE

OF

PICTURES, DRAWINGS, PRINTS,

STATUES and BUSTS in Plaister of Paris,

DONE AT THE

ACADEMY IN THE UNIVERSITY OF GLASGOW.

In this Catalogue is inferted a Collection of Prints, the plates of which are the property of R. and A. Foulis.

Publifhed for the ufe of Subscribers.

PICTURES.

The originals are to be seen at the Academy in Glasgow, except the three following, which are at Hamilton Palace.

SIZES.		PRICES.
		l. s. d.
6 feet 10 inches by 8 feet 10 inches.	COPY of the Convention at Somerfet-houfe, between England, Spain, and Holland, from the famous original in the poffeffion of his Grace the Duke of Hamilton. It contains the portraits of Thomas Earl of Dorfet, Lord High Treafurer, Charles Earl of Nottingham, Lord High Admiral, Charles Earl of Devonfhire, Lord Lieutenant of Ireland, Henry Earl of Northampton, of the Privy Council, Robert Cecil, Firft Secretary of State.—Juan de Velafco, Conftable of Caftile and Duke de Frias, Don Juan de Taffis, Count de Villamediana, Alexandro Rovidio, Senator of Milan.—From the States General, Charles Prince and Count d'Aremberghe, Lord High Admiral, Prefident Richardote, Counfellor of State, Luis Verreyken, Firft Secretary of State. All as large as life.	70 00
7 feet 4 inches by 10 feet 10 inches.	Daniel in the den of lions, after the famous original of Rubens in the poffeffion of his Grace the Duke of Hamilton.	52 10
4 feet 11 inches by 7 feet 10 inches.	The Supper of Emaus, after a picture of Titian's, in the poffeffion of his Grace the Duke of Hamilton.	10 00
7 feet 1 inch by 4 feet 8 1-half inches.	St. Cecilia, after Raphael.	30 00
5 feet 10 inches by 4 feet 5 inches.	Galatea, after Raphael,	22 00
5 feet 8 inches by 7 feet 4 1-half inches.	The Martyrdom of St. Catharine of Alexandria, from a fine original.	15 00
4 feet 6 inches by 5 feet 1 1-half inch.	The four Stages of Life, after Titian.	12 00
5 feet 3 inches by 4 feet 1 1-half inch.	Magdalen with two Angels, after Guido; the fame defign with that in the Barbarini Palace at Rome.	6 00
feet 1 inch by 4 feet 3 inches.	The Judgment of Paris, after de la Hire.	6 06

SIZES.	PICTURES.	PRICES. l. s. d.
3 feet 1 inch by 4 feet 9 3-4th inches.	A view of Glafgow, and of Lord George Sackville's dragoons review'd in the Green.	8 08
3 feet 2 1-half inches by 2 feet 8 inches.	David and Goliah's head, after Guido Cangiacio.	8 00
3 feet 4 inches by 2 feet 7 1-half inches.	Acis and Galatea.	3 03
3 feet 4 inches by 2 feet 8 inches.	A Sybil, after a copy by Boulogne from Guido.	8 08
4 feet 1 1-half inch by 3 feet 2 inches.	Defcent from the Crofs, after an original by Rubens. The large picture is at Antwerp, and juftly admired by all connoiffeurs.	12 12
2 feet 7 inches by 3 feet 4 1-half inches.	The Judgment of Hercules according to the Earl of Shaftesbury's invention.	5 05
2 feet 4 inches by 1 foot 7 inches.	Three children reprefenting Infancy, after Titian.	2 02
3 feet 5 1-half inches by 4 feet 5 inches.	Mutius Scaevola, after Valentini.	5 00
3 feet 9 inches by 5 feet 4 1-half inches.	The Adoration of the Shepherds (all the light reflected from the infant Jefus) after a capital picture by Valentini.	7 07
3 feet 1 inch by 2 feet 1 inch.	Flight into Egypt, after Raphael,	3 03
3 feet 8 inches by 2 feet 9 inches.	A Holy Family, after Carlo Ciniani.	3 03
2 feet high by 3 feet 1 inch.	A Magdalen reading, after Coreggio.	6 06
3 feet 7 inches by 2 feet 4 inches.	Young Tobias receiving his father's bleffing upon his departure, after Imperiali.	2 12 06
3 feet 5 1-half inches by 4 feet 11 inches.	A large Landskip, after de la Hire.	2 10
3 feet by 2 feet 6 inches.	Cupids playing on inftruments, after Coreggio.	2 02
3 feet 6 inches by 2 feet 6 inches.	Our Saviour appearing in the clouds to St. John, from a drawing.	2 10

95

SIZES.	PICTURES.	PRICES.		
		l.	s.	d.
4 feet 7 inches by 3 feet 4 inches.	The Marriage of Cana, an original.	5	05	
4 feet 1 1-half inch by 3 feet 3 3-4th inches.	A Landskip, after Salvator Rofa.	2	00	
	The fame Landskip, fame fize.	1	01	
1 foot 6 inches by 2 feet 6 1-half inches.	A Landskip with a monaftery on a rock in the water, (the idea from Le Clerc) with a white ornamented frame.	2	02	
2 feet by 2 feet 8 inches.	A Landskip, after Sebaftian Bourdon.	1	10	
2 feet by 2 feet 8 inches.	A Flemifh Landskip, after S. L. d. A.	1	10	
1 foot 11 inches by 2 feet 8 1-half inches.	The fame Landskip.	1	00	
3 feet 2 inches by 4 feet 4 1-half inches.	St. Peter in prifon and the Angel who delivers him, after Guido.	3	03	
2 feet by 1 foot 6 1-half inches.	Pyramus and Thifbe, after Nicolas Pouffin.	2	02	
2 feet 5 inches by 2 feet 1 inch.	A Sleeping Cupid, after Nicolas Pouffin.	1	11	06
1 foot 6 inches by 2 feet 1 inch.	A view of Glafgow from below the bridge.	1	11	06
2 feet 1 inch by 2 feet 8 inches.	The bombardment of Bruffels, after Van Euile.	1	05	
2 feet by 3 fett 1 inch.	A view of Govan and the Point-houfe.	1	05	
1 foot 8 inches by 1 foot 2 inches.	Youth reprefented by a young fhepherdefs playing on a flute, after Titian	0	10	
2 feet 1 inch by 2 feet 1 inch.	A portrait, by Peter di Cortona.	1	05	
2 feet 1 inch by 1 foot 7 1-half inches.	A portrait of Raphael.	1	01	
2 feet by 1 foot 5 inches.	A portrait of Titian.	1	01	
1 foot 4 1-half inches by 1 foot 3-4ths of an inch.	The head of the Abbé le Tellier while Ambaffador at Rome to Clement XI.	1	00	

SIZES.	PICTURES.	PRICES.
		l. s. d.
1 foot 11 inches by 1 foot 7 1-half inches.	A portrait of Annibal Caracci.	1 01
feet by 1 foot 7 inches.	A portrait of Rubens.	1 01
	A portrait of Rubens laſt Lady, ſame ſize.	1 01
2 feet 1 inch by 1 foot 7 inches.	St. Peter, after Rubens.	1 00
	St. Paul, after Rubens; ſame ſize.	1 00
2 feet 3 inches by 1 foot 9 inches.	A portrait of Lady Anne Ruthven, wife to Van Dyke, after Van Dyke.	1 01
1 foot 10 inches by 1 foot 6 inches.	A portrait of Rembrant.	1 01
2 feet by 1 foot 8 inches.	Waller's Sachariſſa, after Van Dyke.	1 01
1 foot by 10 inches.	A portrait of Lady Dorothy Sidney, when young, in the character of a nymph of Diana.	0 12
2 feet 7 inches by 1 foot 10 inches.	A portrait after Van Dyke.	1 01
2 feet 1 inch by 1 foot 10 inches.	A Madona and Child, after Raphael.	1 01
1 foot 11 inches by 2 feet 8 inches.	A Waterfall and Landskip.	0 18
2 feet by 3 feet 1 inch.	A view of Cathcart-caſtle.	0 10 06
2 feet by 2 feet 8 inches.	A view of Loch-Lomond.	1 01
	A different view of Loch-Lomond; ſame ſize.	1 01
3 feet by 2 feet.	A waterfall in the Stochie-muir.	0 15
2 feet 9 inches by 2 feet.	Virgin and Child with Angels, after Titian.	1 00
12 3-4th inches by 1 foot 4 1-4th inches.	A Landskip with a mill, and a proſpect of a palace.	0 16
2 feet by 2 feet 8 inches.	A Landskip with a view of a brick-caſtle.	1 01

SIZES.	PICTURES.	PRICES.
		l. s. d.
1 foot 8 1-half inches by 2 feet.	A View of the Rotundo, with a fore-ground from fancy.	0 17
2 feet by 1 foot 7 inches.	Fauſtina, after the Antique.	1 00
2 feet by 1 foot 8 inches.	Lucretia, after Michael Angelo.	0 18 06
1 foot 5 inches by 1 foot 3 inches.	An Old Man ſtudying Aſtronomy, after Gerard Dau.	1 05
	An old Woman reading, its companion, after Do. ſame ſize.	1 05
2 feet by 3 feet.	A Flemiſh Landskip.	1 05
	Its companion; ſame ſize.	1 10
1 foot 11 inches by 1 foot 6 inches.	A portrait of a Fleming, after Rembrant.	0 15
	His wife, its companion, ſame ſize, after Do. The originals are in the Palais Royale.	0 15
1 foot 9 1-half inches by 1 foot 3 1-half inches.	A Coſſack.	0 12
3 feet.	A Landskip, after Jan Sling, a diſciple of Claud Lorrain.	1 11 06
1 foot 2 inches by 11 inches.	Magdalen, a head out of Raphael's Carrying to the Tomb.	1 01
1 foot 3 inches by 12 inches.	Nicodemus, a head from the ſame picture.	1 01
16 1-half inches by 14 inches.	A head of St. Francis.	1 01
2 feet 7 inches by 2 feet.	A St. Catherine reading.	1 05
10 inches by 14.	A Storm at Sea.	0 06
15 inches by 14.	A Storm at Sea, different.	0 06
14 inches by 11	The Virgin's head, from Leon. da Vinci's picture.	0 15
feet 1 inch by 1 foot 7 inches.	St. John Baptiſt.	1 01

N

PICTURES.

SIZES.		PRICES.
		l. s. d.
2 feet 1-half inch by 2 feet 8 1-half inches.	A Piece of Architecture reprefenting a grand palace with a number of figures.	3 03
11 1-half inches by 9 1-half.	Our Saviour's head as taken from Veronica's handkerchief.	0 12
1 foot 11 inches by 2 feet 7 inches.	A Landskip, after Fouquieres.	1 00
2 feet 1 inch by 1 foot 6 3-4th inches.	Our Saviour's head, after Julio Romano.	1 01
2 feet 7 inches by 2 feet 1 1-half inch.	A Landskip with Rocks, after Salvator Rofa.	0 12
10 inches by 8.	A Fleming, after Polbus.	0 12
	A head of Van Dyke, fame fize.	0 12

DRAWINGS.

SIZES and NUMBERS.

1 foot 11 inches by 1 foot 1 1-half inch.	1. Cupid making his Bow, after Correggio, in crayons, with a gilt frame and glazed.	2 02
1 foot 9 inches by 1 foot 4 inches.	2. St. Sebaftian in red chalk, framed and glazed.	1 00
1 foot 9 1-half inches by 2 feet 2 inches.	3. A Pot of Flowers, highly finifhed in red chalk, in an ornamented compartment of invention in black chalk, framed and glazed.	3 03
	4. A Grotefque Ornament in red chalk, framed and glazed.	0 08
	5. Another in black lead, framed and glazed.	0 09
	6. Another in ink, framed and glazed.	0 05
	7. Le Brun's Paffion's, copied with a pen and red ink, at 2s. 6d. each. The fame, when in red chalk, 3s. each.	
	8. Different Views of Glafgow, as well as the country and Seats round it, in pen and ink, from 5 to 15s. each.	
	9. Moft of the above Views, sketched in black chalk, from 1 to 5s. each.	
	10. Landskips, from fancy, sketched in black lead or black chalk, from 1 to 3s.	

NUMBERS.	DRAWINGS.	PRICES.
		l. s. d.
11.	A Drawing in red chalk after a picture of the Madona.	
12.	Our Saviour and St. John by Raphael.	0 10 06
13.	An Angel's head in red chalk.	0 02 06
14.	Head of a Madona in black chalk and blue paper.	0 01 06
15.	Head of Apollo, from fancy.	0 01 06
16.	Head of Adonis, from fancy, in black chalk on blue paper.	0 01 06
17.	Head of Venus, from fancy, in black chalk on blue paper.	0 01 06
18.	Head of Homer, from fancy, as reciting his verfes, in black chalk on blue paper.	0 01 06
19.	Head of the Virgin, from fancy, as repeating the Magnificat, in black chalk on blue paper.	0 01 06
20.	More heads, from fancy, from 1s. to 2s. 6d. each.	
21.	Copied in red chalk from Mr. Strange's Madona after Guido, framed and glazed.	0 10 06
22.	Copied in red chalk from Mr. Strange's Angel after Guido, framed and glazed.	0 10 06
23.	A Madona from Andrea del Sarto, and another from Guercino, both in red chalk, framed and glazed.	0 10 06
24.	Drawings of Portraits, as well as half figures, in pen and ink, or red and black chalk, from 1l. to 1l. 10s.	
25.	Drawings from Bufts, in red or black chalk, from 1s. to 5s.	
26.	Heads from Pictures or Drawings, in red or black chalk, from 1s. to 5s.	
27.	Drawings of Statues, in black or red chalk, from 2s. 6d. to 15s.	
28.	Academy figures from the life, as well as from other drawings, in black or red chalk, from 1s. to 15s. each.	
29.	Drawings after Compofitions of the Capital Mafters, with pen and ink, and with black and red chalk, from 5s. to 3 guineas each.	
30.	Heads in crayons.	
31.	Several other ftudies of heads, hands, legs, and arms, for the ufe of beginners, at various prices.	

PRINTS,

The plates of which are in the possession of R. *and* A. FOULIS.

The number of plates in each set.	HISTORICAL and POETICAL,	PRICES. l. s. d.
6	Reprefenting ftories of the Heathen Gods. Stephanus de Laune fecit, A. D. 1573. 2d. each.	0 01
19	Poetical pieces, befides a frontifpiece, by the fame, at 2d. each.	0 03 04
11	Small poetical pieces of an oval form, by the fame, at 2d. each.	0 01 10
16	Smaller mythological oval pieces from Ovid, by the fame, at 1d. halfpenny each.	0 02
6	Hiftorical pieces, very small, ovals and circles, and when in pairs 3d. the pair, by the fame.	0 00 09
12	Reprefenting the 12 months and figns of the Zodiac, by the fame,	0 02
7	Reprefenting the 7 planets with the figns of the Zodiac, by the fame.	0 01
4	Reprefenting the 4 parts of the world, by the fame,	0 00 08
8	Being 2 fets of peace and war, plenty and famine, by the fame, each fet at	0 00 08
	A Concert of Mufic, after a famous picture by Dominico Zampieri, commonly called Dominichine. C. Duflos fculpfit.	0 00 06
	Aeneas and Anchifes, Creufa and Iulus, flying from Troy, after Dominichino. Jaco fculpfit.	0 00 06
	Menelaus cured by Machaon, all the Grecian Chiefs feem much affected. The ftory is taken from Homer's Iliad.	0 00 06
	Alexander hunting the Lion, and its companion	
	Jafon's landing at Colchis. Both by de la Foffe, at 3d. each.	0 00 06
	The Induftry of Penelope, in the abfence of Ulyffes. Corneille pinxit. Maria Hortomels fculpfit.	0 00 06
	Sappho playing on the lyre and finging in the prefence of the Mufes, Fourbain fculpfit.	0 00 06
	Rhodope, Queen of Egypt, looking at the pyramid fhe had caufed to be built, by the fame.	0 00 06
	They may serve as companions, being all three of the same size.	
	The Triumph of Flora. Pouffin pinxit. M. Hortmel sfculpfit. And	

The number of plates in each set.	PRINTS.		PRICES.	
		l.	s.	d.
	Its companion, The Triumph of Neptune. Mignard pinxit. M. Hortmels fculpfit. 6d. each.	0	01	
2	Converfation Pieces, by de la Hire. Hauffard fculpfit. 4d. each.	0	00	08
	Swifs Guards and others looking over a ftair-cafe, by C. le Brun. In the grand ftair-cafe at Verfailles. Flippart fculpfit.	0	00	04
19	Le Pautre's Drawing-book in 18 plates befides his own portrait.	0	05	
4	The Seafons, with verfes under them, half fheet prints. 4d. each.	0	01	04
16	Rural pieces by Simmonneau, at 3d. each.	0	04	
2	Venus piqued by Love, and its companion			
	Love piqued by Venus, 3d. each.	0	00	06
3	Bacchus, Ceres, and a Bacchante, at 3d. each.	0	00	09
	Venus rifing from the foam of the fea; a fheet print.	0	00	06
	Aurora preceding the Sun. Le Soeur invenit.	0	00	06
	Daphne flying from Apollo. Hoüaffe pinxit. Flipart fculpfit.	0	00	04
6	Pieces of fcenery by Chauveau, viz.			
	1. The Star of Venus, with a beautiful varied fcene of architecture.			
	2. Aeolus, with a fine rural fcene of architecture.			
	3. Juno in her chariot, with a noble fcene of architecture.			
	4. Her taking place of Cepheus, a grand fcene of architecture.			
	5. Melpomene meeting the chariot of the Sun, a rural fcene with a large grotto.			
	6. Perfeus and Andromeda, a terrible fcene of rocks in the fea, with a diftant view. 3d. each.	0	01	06
4	Reprefenting a Quack Doctor.	0	00	08
5	Drolls and Caricaturas.	0	00	10
8	Callot's Beggars, 4 large and 4 fmaller. 3d. each.	0	02	
	The Hours of the Day, a ceiling piece. Blanchard pinxit. Simonneau fculpfit.	0	00	06
	Jupiter and Prometheus, idem. Mignard pinxit. C. Depuis fculpfit.	0	00	06
	Its companion, Pfyche prefented to the Gods. idem. by fame.	0	00	0

PRINTS.

Number of plates in each set		Prices l. s. d.
	Mars throwing the thunder with emblems of war. idem. Le Brun pinxit. M. Hortmels fculpfit.	
	Its companion, Peace with its emblems. idem. by fame. 6d. each.	0 01
	Time carrying away Truth. idem. A fheet print. N. Pouffin.	0 01
	Time difcovering Truth, with a motto of eternity, envy, and defpair. idem. A fheet print. N. Pouffin.	0 01
	Mercury attending and hovering over the Arts and Sciences. idem. Corneille pinxit. M. Hortmels fculpfit.	0 00 06
44	Reprefenting 87 converfation pieces, different attitudes and compofitions. French.	0 03 08
37	Women of different nations, by Hollar.	0 03 08
4	The Seafons, with French and Englifh names. 3d. each.	0 01
4	The Seafons, by Vignon. 3d. each	0 01 00
5	The Senfes, by the fame.	0 01 03
4	The 4 Parts of the World, by the fame.	0 01
4	The Elements, by the fame.	0 01
4	The 4 Parts of the Day, by the fame.	0 01
4	Paris and the 3 Goddeffes, by the fame.	0 01
30	Paris Cries and Cuftoms.	0 00 04
	Iphigenia.	0 02 06
	The Miffifippi, a fatyrical piece.	0 00 04
	Harpalice delivering her father Lycurgus. Vignon pinx. M. Hortmels fcul.	0 00 06
	Europa, an etching by Cofin, after Le Fage.	0 00 01
	Heroic Virtue victorious over Vice. And	
	The Senfual Man. both after Corregio. at 4d. each.	0 00 08
	Astronomy. Raphael pinxit in Vaticano. N. Boquet fculpfit.	0 00 06
	Apollo preferred to Marfyas, from the fame, by Boquet.	0 00 05

HISTORICAL and SACRED.

	Adam and Eve tempted by the ferpent, from Raphael, by Boquet.	0 00 06
	The Judgment of Solomon, from the fame, by Boquet. All the four are companions.	0 00 06
36	Reprefenting the hiftory of the Old Teftament, by Steph. de Laune.	0 03
11	Reprefenting the hiftory of the Old Teftament in oval forms, by the fame.	0 01

The number of plates in each set.	PRINTS.	PRICES. l. s. d.
3	More of the New Teftament, by Picart.	6 00 06
8	Reprefenting the 4 Evangelifts, and 4 other remarkable paffages of Scripture. chez Gallays. 1d. halfpenny each.	0 01
10	Reprefenting the chief ftages of our Saviour's Paffion, his refurrection, &c. by H. Goltzius. 3d. each. in all	0 02 06
	The Marriage of Cana, by the fame. the fame fize.	0 00 03
	Our Saviour walking on the fea and fupporting St. Peter, who is ready to fink, by R. Sadler, jun.	0 00 06
	A dead Chrift with angels weeping; ufually called a *Pietà*. De la Hire invenit et fecit.	0 00 06
	A Mater Dolorofa, its companion, by the fame.	0 00 06
	Plates invented by Annibal Carraccio, and engraved by S. Guillain;	
	1. Our Saviour.	0 00 02
	2. The Affumption of the Virgin.	0 00 02
	3. St. John the Baptift.	0 00 02
	4. St. John the Evangelift.	0 00 02
	5. St. Laurence.	0 00 02
	6. St. Francis.	0 00 02
	St. Jerom meditating on the laft Judgment, an angel by him. Jof. Heintz pinxit. L Kilian fculpfit.	0 01
	Jofeph and Potiphar's Wife. Albano pinxit. M. Hortmels fculpfit.	0 00 04
	The Virgin, our Saviour, and St. John, alluding to that part of Scripture where St. John accounts himfelf unworthy to loofe our Saviour's fandals. De la Hire inv. et fecit.	0 00 06
	The Virgin and St. Jofeph, our Saviour pulling a palm branch out of their hands, by the fame.	0 00 06
	The Virgin and Child, with angels fupporting and carrying the crofs, by the fame.	0 00 06
	The Virgin and Child with St. Catharine. Van Dyke inv. Ragot fculp.	0 00 06
	The Virgin and Child. Stella in. Couvay fculpfit.	0 00 06
	The Virgin and our Saviour. Carlo Maratti inv. Dormeillier fculpfit.	0 00 04
	The Virgin and Babe. Gallays excudit.	0 00 03
	The Virgin, our Saviour, and St. John, by Chauveau.	0 00 06

The number of plates in each set.	PRINTS.	PRICES.
		l. s. d.

15	Reprefenting our Saviour, St. John Baptift, and the 12 Apoftles. Gallays excudit. 2d. each. the fet at	0	02
	The Crucifixion, after Le Brun.	0 00	06
	Our Saviour taken down from the crofs. N. Pouffin pinxit. F. Chauveau fculpfit.	0	01
	The Carrying to the Tomb. Fred. Baroccius pinxit. Sadler fculp.	0	01
	The fame fubject. Tintoret pinxit. L. Kilian fculpfit.	0	01
	The Refurrection of our Saviour. P. Cagliare Veronenfis pinxit. L. Kilian fculpfit.	0 00	09
	The Raifing of Lazarus. J. Palma pinxit. L. Kilian fculpfit.	0 00	09
	The Martyrdom of a Saint. P. Cagliari inv. P. Brebiette fculpfit.	0 00	03
14	Different fized facred hiftories, from 2d to 6d each.		
14	Different reprefentations of the Crucifixion, from 1d. to 4d.		
50	Saints and Religious Perfons, different fizes, from 1d. to 6d. each.		
16	Prints on 8 plates, of the fame fize, reprefenting faints and facred hiftory, at 3d. a pair.	0	02
32	Prints on 15 plates, different fizes, moftly fmall, facred fubjects. One of the plates contains 4 prints, all fmall, from 1d. to 4d. each.		
3.	The laft Supper, Afcenfion, and laft Judgment, at 4d.	0	01
6	Plates reprefenting the hiftory of Tobias by Maurpech. 3d. each.	0 01	06
12	Reprefenting the Hiftory of the Old and New Teftament, on large half fheets, Gio. Ben. Caftiglione inv. C. Mace fculp. 6d. each.	0	05
3	Reprefenting different facts in St. Anthony's life. A. Carrach invenit. S. G. fculpfit.	0 00	06
	Zippora circumcifeth her fon.	0	01
	St. Jerom tempted in the Wildernefs. Dominico Zampieri detto Dominichino pinxit.	0	01
	Our Saviour permitting him to be whipt as a Ciceronian, a vifion, by the fame.	0	01
	The Sacrament of Baptifm, by the fame. All fheet prints.	0	01

The pictures of the above three prints are to be feen at St. Andrew's Church at Rome.

PRINTS.

Number of plates in each set		Prices s. d.
3	The fame three in fmall. 6d. each.	1 6
10	Sacred Emblems, at 3d. each.	2 6
	The Virgin and Child. Blanchard pinx. Duret fculpfit.	0 6
10	Our Saviour, the Virgin, 4 Evangelifts, and fome Apoftles; ovals with garlands of flowers round them. 2d. halfpenny each.	2
2	Jefus and Mary, 3d. each.	0 6
	Our Saviour. Jac. Blanchard pinxit. Petr. Daret fculp.	0 6
	The Virgin, by the fame hand. Companions and half-fheet prints.	0 6
	St. Francifcus de Paulo. half-length. John Lenfant fculp.	0 6
	A Magdalen, by Jof. Ribiera detto. Spagnoletto.	0 8

The following is a Collection of Whole-length Figures.

	An Ecco Homo. D. Humbelot inv. Ae. Rouffelet fecit.	0 6
2	Jefus Amabilis and Mater Amabilis. C. le Brun inv. Rouffelet fculpfit. 6d. each.	1
	Regina Martyrum. Rouffelet inv. et fecit.	0 6
	St. Jofeph. De la Hire invenit. Couvay fecit.	0 6
	St. John the Baptift. by the fame. Rouffelet fecit.	0 6
	St. John the Evangelift. by the fame. Rouffelet fecit.	0 6
	St. Auguftin. C. le Brun invenit. Rouffelet fecit.	0 6
	St. Agnes. De la Hire invenit. Rouffelet fecit.	0 6
	St. Benedictus. by the fame. Rouffelet fecit.	0 6
	St. Francis. by the fame. Rouffelet fecit.	0 6
	St. Sebaftian. by the fame. Rouffelet fecit.	0 6
	St. Scholaftica. by the fame. Rouffelet fecit.	0 6
	St. Genevieve. by the fame. Rouffelet fecit.	0 6
	St. Bruno. C. le Brun invenit. Rouffelet fecit.	0 6
	St. Roch. Vignon invenit. Rouffelet fecit.	0 6
	St. Carolus Baromeus. by the fame. Rouffelet fecit.	0 6
	St. Claudius. by the fame. Couvay fecit.	0 6
	St. Urfula. by the fame. Rouffelet fecit.	0 6
	St. Gulielmus. by the fame. Couvay fecit.	0 6
	St. Carolus Magnus. by the fame. Couvay fecit.	0 6
	St. Lewis. by the fame. Rouffelet fecit.	0 6
	St. Catherine. by the fame. Rouffelet fecit.	0 6
	St. Anthony. by the fame. Couvay fecit.	0 6
	St. Nicolas. by the fame. Couvay fecit.	0 6
	St. Helena. by the fame. Rouffelet fecit.	0 6

106

The number of plates in each set.

PRINTS.

PRICES.

		s.	d.
	St. Hieronymus. Auguſtine Carrach invenit. C. Galle ſculpſit.	0	6
	St. Mary Magdalen. Blanchard pinxit. Stella ſculpſit.	0	6
	St. Bernard. by C. le Brun. Rouſſelet fecit.	0	6
	A Guardian Angel. Couvay fecit.	0	6
	All the above are upon half ſheets.		
	St. Philip the Apoſtle.	0	8

STATUES.

		s.	d.
20	Small Statues on ſeven plates. Joannes de Laune filius del. Stephanus pater ſculpſit A. D. 1573.	1	
13	Repreſenting Minerva or Genius, Science, and 11 Arts and Sciences, ovals. by Stephanus de Laune.	1	
8	Repreſenting the Cardinal and Heroic Virtues, ovals. by ſame.	0	8
32	Heathen Gods and Demigods. by Caracci. 2d. each.	4	
	The Rape of the Sabines, by John de Boulogne. Natoire del. Deſplaces ſculpſit.	0	6
	The Bath of Apollo, by Girardon and Regnaudin. Thomaſin delin. et ſculpſit.	1	6
2	The Horſes of the Sun, by Gerin, in two views. Thomaſin del. et ſculp.		
	The Triumph of Apollo, by Thierry. And		
	The Triumph of Amphitrite, its companion, by the ſame. Thomaſin del. et ſculpſit.	1	6
	The ſtatue of Victory or Fame a horſe-back, by Coiſveau. And		
	The ſtatue of Mercury a horſeback, its companion, by the ſame. Thomaſin del. et ſculpſit.	1	6
	Theſe two laſt are placed in the grand-entry to the Tuilleries.		
	Diana and Endymion, by Thierry. Thomaſin ſculpſit.	1	
	Victory over the Empire. Thomaſin ſculpſit.	0	4
	Victory over Spain. Surugue ſculpſit.	0	4
2	Peace and Plenty. Surugue ſculpſit.	0	8
12	The twelve Months. C. le Brun invenit. engraved by Surugue and others.	4	
4	Repreſenting the Seaſons, by Picart.	1	
4	Repreſenting the 4 parts of the Day, by the ſame.	1	6
4	Repreſenting the 4 parts of the World, by the ſame.	1	
3	The Rape of Proſerpine, a ſhepherdeſs, and Flora, by the ſame. 4d. each.	1	

PRINTS,

The number of plates in each set.

PRICES.

ORNAMENTS, *most of them of use for Chasers, Stucco-men and Goldsmiths.*

		s.	d.
18	Trophies, Battle-pieces, and Hunting-pieces, by Stephanus de Laune.	2	3
12	Ornaments, emblematical of the arts and fciences, 6 of the fciences with light grounds, by de Laune.	1	
6	Square fmall emblematical ornaments for a Bible, by the fame.	0	6
6	Square fmall emblematical ornaments, poetical or hiftorical, by the fame.	0	6
7	Various fhaped grotefque ornaments, by the fame.	0	7
8	Oval ornaments, grotefque, by the fame.	0	8
3	Larger ovals, reprefenting Bacchanals of Cupids, by the fame.	0	3
3	Smaller ovals, reprefenting grotefques, by the fame.	0	3
4	Circular grotefques.	0	4
2	Ovals larger than any above-mentioned, by Steph. de Laune.	0	2
10	Plates, containing feveral pieces on each plate, of various forms and fizes. A book for the ufe of chafers and goldfmiths. Jacques Collen inv. et. fc.		
16	Sacred emblematical ornaments, of various fizes, by different hands, 3 or 4 on a plate, from 1d. to 6d. each.		
11	Plates of various larger ornament, for the ufe of ftucco-men or carpenters, 2 or 3 on the fame plates, by different hands, from 3d. to 4d. each.		
6	Ornamented ceiling-pieces, with a frontifpiece, by le Moyn, at 4d. each.	2	
	A fheet ornament, and two others fmaller, for placing a print or infcription into. 6d. each.		
	A Chinefe Tree, on two fheets, with great variety of work.	2	0

PORTRAITS.

	s.	d.
Charles XII. King of Sweden, at full length.	0	3
Huygens Engraved by Edelinck.	1	
Michael le Tellier, Chancellor of France. F. Voet pinxit. Edelinck, fculp.	1	
Guido Patin Parifienfis Medicus et Profeffor Regius. A. Maffon prinx. et fc.	0	6

PRINTS.

The number of plates in each set.

		s.	d.
	Valentin Conrart, Secretary to the French Academy, &c. C. le Fevre pinx. L. Coffin fculp.	1	
	Caffini the famous Aftronomer, with a view of the Obfervatory at Paris. L. Coffin fculpfit.	0	6
	J. D. Auvergne Parifienfis, Arabicae linguae Profeffor Regius. J. Lenfan ad vivum faciebat.	0	6
	Malbranche. Rochfort fculpfit.	0	6
	Fra. Chauveau of the Royal Academy of painting and fculpture. Le Fevre pinxit. L. Coffin fecit.	0	6
	Fr. Herard, Chirurgeon of Paris, famous for the operation of the trepan and others. F. Siere pinxit. L. Coffin fculpfit.	0	6
	J. Doujat, Dean of the French Academy, and Hiftoriographer to Lewis XIV. F. Sierre pinxit. L. Coffin fculpfit.	0	6
	Claudius de Hervy, Aedile of Paris, Anna Rouffelet, his wife, Johannes de Hervy, Regi a Confiliis, } Lochon fculpfit.	0	9
	Johanna de Hervy. Alzenbach fculpfit.	0	3
	Maria Depardieu, uxor nobilis Aegidii Morelli. Lochon poft mortem delin. et fculpfit.	0	3
	Claudius Morellus Abbas, frater Aegidii. by the fame.	0	3
	Carolus Morellus. by the fame.	0	3
	Fredericus Morellus, Profeffor and Royal Interpreter.	0	3
	Gulielmus Blancus, Chamberlain to Sextus IV. Tho. de Jeu fculpfit.	0	3
	Armand Jean Boutilier, Premier Abbé de la Trappe.	0	6
	Lewis Antoine de Noailles, Cardinal and Archbifhop of Paris.	0	6
2	An old Man and his Wife, Mifers.	0	4
44	Portraits of French nobility, gentlemen and Ladies. 2d. each.	7	4
12	Heads by Rembrant copied.	2	
	The Dauphin's family.	0	4
	Lewis IX. King of France.	0	3

LANDSKIPS, BEASTS, and BIRDS &c.

8	Large views, by Hollar. 4d. each.	2	8
12	Smaller views by the fame, 2d.	2	
9	Views of Verfailles, from 3d. to 6d. each.		
	An old Ruin.	0	2
6	Country pleafuring and amufements, by le Pautre. 2d. each.	1	
4	Dutch country merriments, by Teniers. 2d. each.	0	8

The number of plates in each set.	PRINTS.	PRICES. s. d.
2	Cattle-pieces, Camels, &c. after M. Rosa. 2d. each.	0 4
2	Landskips with figures, by Perelle. 4d. each.	0 8
5	Cattle-pieces, by Berghem. 4d. each.	1 8
3	Landskips with figures and cattle, by Paul van Somer. 3d. each.	0 9
7	Landskips with figures bathing, etched by Count Caylus. 1d each.	0 7
6	Pieces of birds. 1d. halfpenny each.	0 9
6	Baskets of fruit and flowers. 1d. halfpenny each.	0 9
	A Landskip, Flemifh.	0 4

The following are plates which have been engraved at Glasgow. Among the first things were copied as follows;

1ft. *By* ROBERT PAUL.

A view, with a funeral monument.	0 1½
A View near Chelfea.	0 2
A Boar-hunting, after Silvefter.	0 2
Ruins, after le Clerc.	0 3
A Landskip with ruins.	0 3
A monaftry curioufly fituated upon a rock in the water, from le Clerk.	0 3
A fmall Deer-hunting, with a view of a palace, from Silvefter.	0 4
A boy holding up a basket of fruit, reprefenting the Fertility of the Earth, after Diepenbeck.	0 6

2d. *By* JAMES MAXWELL.

Ovidius Nafo, from Bellori.	0 3
Hippocrates, after Sandrart.	0 3
Sophocles, after the fame.	0 3
A head of Jofeph, after Jacomo Frey's print of Joseph and Potiphar's wife, from Carlo Morat.	0 2
The lame man's head, etched after Raphael.	0 2
A Mufe, from the Mufeum Florentinum.	0 6
Appollo, a ftatue. M. F.	1

3d. *By* JOHN LAWSON.

A head of the Virgin, from Raphael.	0 2
A head of Horace, from Pine, after the antique.	0 4
A head of Fenelon, Archbifhop of Cambray, from a fmall print.	0 4
A head of Germanicus, a gem. M. F.	0 3
Virgo Victrix.	0 2
The Amazon Penthefilea flain by Achilles. M. F.	0 5
Diomedes and Glaucus exchanging fhields. M. F.	0 6
Diana, a ftatue. M. F.	0 9

PRINTS.

The number of plates in each set.

PRICES.

s. d.

By JAMES MITCHELL.

		s.	d.
9	Small heads after the antique, viz. Roma, Numa, Junius, Brutus, Pompey, Julius Caefar, M. Antony, M. Varo, Brutus the Younger, Octavius afterwards Augustus. 3d. each.	2	3
	Jupiter's head, a gem. M. F.	0	3
	A Conquering Wreftler. M. F.	0	3
	Penthefilea dying, fuftained by Achilles. M. F.	0	4
	A head of Horace.	0	3
	An Amazon. M. F.	0	3
	Jupiter, a ftatue.	0	6
	Hercules and Iole, a gem. M. F.	0	6

5th. *By* WILLIAM JAMESON.

	s.	d.
A head out of Jacomo Frey's print of a Holy Family by Carlo Morat.	0	3
A head of St. John.	0	4
A head of Socrates. very fmall.	0	2
A head of Aefculapius, a gem. M. F.	0	3
A head of Medufa, a gem. M. F.	0	3
A head of Hercules, when young, a gem. M. F.	0	3
Hercules Victor, a gem. M. F.	0	3
Roma, with a Cornucopia, a gem. M. F.	0	3
Another Roma, a gem. M. F.	0	3
A head of Ulyffes, a gem. M. F.	0	2
Anacreon.	0	2
Alexander the Great.	0	2
Socrates.	0	2
Aventinus fon of Hercules.	0	2
Antinous.	0	2
Head of Virgil.	0	3
Head of Horace.	0	3
A head of an Amazon. M. F.	0	3
A trumpeter. M. F.	0	3
Livia.	0	3
Octavia.	0	3
Victory. M. F.	0	3
A ftatue of Endymion. M. F.	1	

VIEWS *taken by* ROBERT PAUL.

	s.	d.
Profpect of the entry to the Black-fryars Church at Glafgow.	0	3
View of the middle-walk in the College-garden.	0	3

PRINTS.

	PRICES.
	s. d.
View from the South of the Cathedral Church at Glafgow.	0
View of St. Andrew's Church, which was lately built at Glafgow, from the battlements of the Town-houfe.	0 4
View of the Cathedral Church at Glafgow from the Weft, larger.	0 9
View of the fame from the North, larger.	0 9
View of the fame from the South-eaft.	0 4
View of the Banks of Clyde from York-hill.	0 6
View of the Bridge from the Old Wind-mill.	0 3
View of Glafgow from Anderfton.	0 6

Will soon be ready.

The Farnefe Gallery by Annibal Carracci, without the ornaments.

It is likewise proposed to print, in a small form, adorned with the elegant Plates of Sebastian Le Clerc, the following Italian Poets.

La Gierufalemme Liberata di Torquato Taffo, with 20 plates, befides the frontifpiece and the author's head.
L'Aminta di Taffo, with 6 plates, befides a frontifpiece and his head.
Il Paftor Fido di Guarini, with 6 plates, befides a frontifpiece.
La Filli di Sciro, with 6 plates, befides a frontifpiece.
L'Adone dell Marino, with 19 plates, befides a frontifpiece.

STATUES in PLAISTER of PARIS, moulded at Glafgow.

*Those marked with a * were modelled there.*

SIZES.		PRICES.	PRICES.
		l. s. d.	l. s. d.
	The Gladiator Borghefe, fame fize with the famous Antique. The real length of the figure is 6 feet 6 inches, but the height from the ground is only 5 feet 6 inches.	8 00 0	
	The fame in lead.	15 15 0	
feet 7 inches long and 10 inches in height.	A Cupid lying covering himfelf with a piece of drapery, by Fiamingo ; And its companion, by the fame. 15s. each.	1 10 0	
	The above two when varnifhed. 20s. each.	2 00 0	
	They are proper for putting over architraves or cornices on door-heads.		

BUSTS

SIZES.	SMALLER STATUES.	PRICES. Unvarnifhed. l. s. d.	PRICES. Varnifhed. l. s. d.
2 feet 4 1-half inches high.	Apollo.	0 10 0	0 13 0
2 feet 4 inches.	The Dancing Faun.	0 10 0	0 13 0
2 feet 4 1-half inches.	* The Gladiator Borghefe.	0 10 0	0 13 0
2 feet 2 inches.	Leda and the Swan.	0 10 0	0 13 0
2 feet.	Venus of Medici.	0 10 0	0 13 0
1 foot 10 1-half inches.	Amphitrite.	0 9 0	0 12 0
1 foot 9 1-half inches.	Flora.	0 7 0	0 10 0
1 foot 8 1-half inches.	Antinous.	0 7 0	0 10 0
1 foot 8 1-half inches.	A young Faun piping.	0 7 0	0 10 0
1 foot 8 inches.	Antaeus.	0 7 0	0 10 0
1 foot 9 1-half inches.	An anatomical figure.	0 7 0	0 10 0
1 foot 9 inches.	Hercules and Antaeus wreftling.	0 15 0	1 1 0
1 foot 9 inches.	The fame in a different pofture.	0 15 0	1 1 0
	Mercury flying.	0 5 0	0 3 6
1 foot 2 inches.	Mercury leaning.	0 4 0	0 6 0
1 foot 2 inches.	Apollo.	0 4 0	0 6 0
1 foot 2 inches.	Venus.	0 4 6	0 6 0

MODERN STATUES.

1 foot 8 inches.	Shakefpear, with a monument.	0 7 6	0 10 6
1 foot 9 inches.	Milton, with a monument.	0 7 6	0 10 6
1 foot 8 inches.	Another Milton.	0 6 0	0 8 6
13 1-half inches.	Shakefpear, with a monument.	0 4 0	0 4 6
13 1-half inches.	Milton, with a monument.	0 4 0	0 4 6
13 1-half inches.	Pope, with a monument.	0 4 0	0 4 6
13 1-half inches.	Gay, with a monument.	0 4 0	0 4 6
15 inches.	Autumn or Bacchus.	0 2 6	0 3 6
15 inches.	Winter or a Skating Boy.	0 2 6	0 3 6

BUSTS, as large as life, from the Antique.

2 feet 7 inches.	Antoninus.	1 11 6	1 16 6
2 feet 3 3-4th inches.	Jupiter.	1 1 0	1 5 0
2 feet 3 1-half inches.	Homer.	1 1 0	1 5 0
2 feet 2 3-4th inches.	Sylla.	1 1 0	1 5 0
2 feet 2 1-half inches.	Caracalla.	1 1 0	1 5 0
2 feet 1 inch.	Veftal Virgin.	1 1 0	1 5 0
2 feet 1 inch.	Fauftina.	1 1 0	1 5 0
1 foot 11 inches.	Cicero.	0 18 0	1 1 0
1 foot 11 1-half inches.	Seneca.	0 18 0	1 1 0

BUSTS.

SIZES.		PRICES. Unvarnifhed. l. s. d.	PRICES. Varnifhed. l. s. d.
1 foot 10 1-half inches.	Nero, young.	0 12 0	0 15 0
1 foot 11 1-half inches.	Annius Verus.	0 12 0	0 15 0
1 foot 6 1-half-inches.	M. Aurelius Antoninus, young.	0 12 0	0 15 0

Less than Life.

1 foot 5 inches.	A Madonna.	0 7 0	0 9 0
1 foot 6 1-half inches.	Apollo of Belvidere.	0 6 0	0 8 0
1 foot 6 inches.	Aefculapius.	0 6 0	0 8 0
1 foot 5 1-half inches.	* Homer.	0 6 0	0 8 0
1 foot 5 inches.	Plato.	0 7 0	0 9 0
1 foot 6 1-half inches.	Virgil.	0 7 0	0 9 0
1 foot 5 inches.	Cicero.	0 7 0	0 9 0
1 foot 8 inches.	* M. Aurelius Antoninus.	0 7 0	0 9 0
1 foot 4 1-half inches.	* Veftal Virgin.	0 5 0	0 6 6
1 foot 4 1-half inches.	* Fauftina.	0 5 0	0 6 6

MODERN BUSTS.

1 foot 11 1-half inches.	* King of Pruffia.	0 10 0	0 12 0
1 foot 8 1-half inches.	* The Prince of Wales.	0 6 0	0 8 0
1 foot 5 inches.	* Raphael.	0 6 0	0 8 0
1 foot 5 inches.	* Annibal Caracci.	0 6 0	0 8 0
1 foot 5 1-half inches.	* Sir Walter Rawleigh.	0 4 0	0 5 6
1 foot 5 1-half inches.	* Shakefpear.	0 6 0	0 8 0
1 foot 5 1-half inches.	* Milton.	0 4 0	0 5 6
1 foot 5 inches.	Dryden.	0 6 0	0 8 0
1 foot 5 inches.	Newton.	0 6 0	0 8 0
1 foot 6 inches.	Prior.	0 6 0	0 8 0
1 foot 4 1-half inches.	Pope.	0 6 0	0 8 0

SMALL BUSTS.

12 1-half inches.	Livy.	0 3 0	0 4 0
14 1-half inches.	* A Madonna.	0 2 6	0 3 6
13 1-half inches.	* The Angel Gabriel.	0 2 6	0 3 6
1 foot.	A head of Cupid, with a pedeftal, moulded on an original modelling of Fiamingo.	0 5 0	0 6 0
1 foot 1 inch.	A head of Pan, } *for putting into the cornices of*	0 4 0	0 5 0
12 1-half inches.	A head of Silenus, } *chimney-pieces, or door-heads.*	0 4 0	0 5 0
6 1-half in. by 6 1-half	A Boy fitting, after Fiamingo.	0 1 6	0 2 0
12 1-half inches by 15.	* A Boy fitting, modelled after the former.	0 2 6	0 3 0

P

BUSTS.

SIZES.		PRICES. Unvarnifhed. l. s. d.	PRICES. Varnifhed. l. s. d.
11 1-half inches.	Venus.	0 2 0	0 2 6
11 1-half inches.	Flora.	0 2 0	0 2 6
11 1-half inches.	Apollo.	0 2 0	0 2 6
11 inches.	Leda.	0 2 0	0 2 6
11 1-half inches.	Cicero.	0 2 6	0 3 0
1 foot.	Virgil.	0 2 6	0 3 0
11 inches.	Shakefpear.	0 2 0	0 2 6
11 inches.	Milton.	0 2 0	0 2 6
1 foot.	* King of Pruffia.	0 2 6	0 3 0
1 foot.	Vandyke.	0 2 0	0 2 6
11 inches.	Antoninus.	0 2 0	0 2 6
10 inches.	Fauftina.	0 1 6	0 2 0
9 inches.	Cicero.	0 1 6	0 2 0
9 inches.	Demofthenes.	0 1 6	0 2 0
8 1-half inches.	A Satyr.	0 1 6	0 2 0
8 inches.	Cleopatra.	0 1 0	0 1 6
8 inches.	Lucretia.	0 1 0	0 1 6

URNS AND ORNAMENTED BRACKETS.

	Large Urns.	0 5 0	0 7 0
	Small Urns.	0 1 0	0 1 6
	A Bracket for the large ftatues of Shakefpear or Milton.	0 4 0	0 5 0
	A bracket for any of the middle-fized bufts or ftatues.	0 7 6	0 10 0
	2 Other Brackets for the fame (companions) both at	0 7 6	0 10 0
	A Bracket for the fmalleft ftatues.	0 1 0	0 1 6
	A Bracket for the fmall bufts.	0 1 0	0 1 6

BASRELIEVOS's.

		Plaifter.	Wax.
5 inches by 4.	Dr. Francis Hutchefon.	0 2 6	0 7 6
5 inches by 8.	Ceres.	0 3 0	0 10 0
5 inches by 8.	A Bacchanal.	0 3 0	0 10 0
6 inches by 8.	Judith with Holophernes' head.	0 3 0	0 10 0
5 inches by 8.	A fleeping Venus.	0 3 0	0 10 0

SIZES.	BUSTS cut in Stone.	PRICES.
		l. s. d.
1 foot 11 inches.	Cicero.	5 0 0
1 foot 11 1-half inches.	Seneca.	4 0 0
1 foot 8 1-4th inches.	Livy.	3 0 0

N.B. Any perfon may have a ftatue or buft done in Paris-plaifter, after a picture, drawing, or print.

As the copies of the Congrefs at Somerfet-houfe and Daniel in the Den of Lions were done at Hamilton, at a great expence, if any perfon chufes other copies, they will be done at a cheaper rate. The copies in general are valued according to the hands who do them, fo that a copy of the fame picture will be fold higher or lower according as it is done.

ORIGINAL PAPERS.

ORIGINAL PAPERS.

No. I.

Propofals for erecting a bookfellers fhop and a printing prefs within the Univerfity of Glafgow, [1713].

It's needlefs to fhew how neceffary and advantagious a well furnifh'd fhop with books, paper, pens, ink, &c. or a printing prefs within the Univerfity will be, or to obferve that no Learned Society has ever flourifh'd to any pitch without thofe helps. The common practice of all famous Seminarys of Learning makes this matter of fact evident, and our own experience here fufficiently confirms whatever can be s^d. in its favours, every day teaches us what difficulty there is to get the books that are abfolutely neceffary for the fcholars of all forts, and how much we are impof'd upon when we gett y^m. And as to a printing prefs, the fingle confideration of our being obliged to go to Ed^r. in order to gett one fheet right printed makes out the abfolut neceffity of one.

In order to have the Univerfity well accommodated with books, and a printing prefs, It is propofed that before the next feffions of the College there fhall be a well furnifh'd fhop erected, with books of all forts, paper, paper-books, pens, ink, ink-horns, fealing wax, and all other things fold either in a bookfellers or ftationers shop, as alfo that fometime within four years after whitfunday next there fhall be a printing prefs erected, with neceffary funts and other materials for printing Heb: Greek, and Latin, upon the conditions and manner after fpecified, viz.

1. That the Undertaker fhall be immediately declared Univerfity bookfeller and printer, and that all the priviledges, immunitys, and advantages, which the Univerfity can beftow on a bookfeller or printer fhall be affigned to the s^d. undertaker and his affegneys whatfomever, and that for 40 years.

2ly. That a convenient fhop and warehoufe within the College be allowed gratis to the s^d. undertaker, and that the s^d. fhop fhall be floord with dales and fhelves, tables, a brace and chimney, and Large chace window putt in it at the expence of the Univerfity.

3ly. That when the printing prefs fhall be erected the Univerfity furnifh a convenient printing houfe, and for laying up books printed and drying the paper, &c.

4ly. [deleted].

5. That the Undertaker be obliged either to erect the prefs within the time above mentioned, or forfeit his priviledges of bookfeller and printer.

Since the earlier part of this volume was printed, the writer has been favoured by William Motherwell, Esq. with the following extracts from the Records of the Town Council:—

20 April 1641.	Item to George Anderfoune prenter his Zeirs penfioune	lxvj.^{lib}	xiij.^{s}	iiij.^{d}
12 Nov. 1642.	Item to George Anderfone prenter	lxvij.^{lib}	xiij.^{s}	iiij.^{d}
″ ″ 1643.	Item to Georg Anderfone prenter	lxvij.^{lib}	xiij.^{s}	iiij.^{d}
17 Feby. 1645.	Item to Georg Anderfone	lxvij.	xiij.^{s}	iiij.
7 March 1646.	Item to George Anderfoune printer	lxvij.	xiij.	iiij.^{d}
29 May 1647.	Item to George Anderfoune printer of feall	lxvij.	xiij.^{s}	iiij.^{d}
″ ″ ″	Item to George Anderfoun printer for service	vj.^{l}	xiij.^{s}	iiij.^{d}
11 March 1648.	Item to George Anderfoun prenter	xxxiij.	vj.^{s}	iiij.^{d}

The entries in the year 1647 seem to indicate that, besides his pension, Anderson was paid for his "fervice" by the town.

No. II.

Agreement Between the Colledge of Glafgow and Donald Govane yor, 1715.

ATT the Colledge of Glafgow the Tenth day of January J^m vij^c and ffifteen years It is agreed and finally ended Between the perfons parties underwryten They are to fay Mr. John Stirling Principal of the Univerfitie of Glasgow, Mr. John Simpfon profeffor of Theologie y^r, Mr. William Forbes profeffor of Law, Mr. John Johnftoun profeffor of phyfick, Mrs. Gerfhom Carmichael and John Loudoun profeffors of philofophie, Mr. Alexander Dunlop profeffor of Greek, Mr. Andrew Rofs, profeffor of Humanitie, Mr. Charles Morthlan [d] profeffor of the orientall Languages, Mr. Robert Simpfon profeffor of Matthematicks, and Mr. Robert Dick profeffor of philofophie y^r with the fpeciall advice and confent of Sir John Maxwell of Netherpollok Knight and Barronett one of the Senators of the Colledge of Juftice Rector, And of Mr. John Hamiltoun one of the Ministers of the Gofpell in Glafgow Dean of ffacultie of the faid Univerfitie on the one part And Donald Govan younger merchant in Glafgow and printer on the other part In manner following Thats to fay fforafmuchas The faid Univerfitie Hath Nominated Conftituted and Appoynted And hereby Nominatts Conftituts and Appoynts the faid Donald Govane Printer to the faid Univerfitie and that for all the years and space of feven years And sua long thereafter as the faid Univerfitie fhall pleafe provyding alwayes he affign not the s^d priviledge of printer to the Univerſitie to any without Confent of the ffacultie And that no book bear to be printed by him or his Deput as printer to the faid Univerſitie Unlefs he be allowed by the faid ffacultie To defign himfelf fo In the Title page of the books And the faid Univerſitie obleidge them and y^r. fucce^{rs}. in offices To ffurnifh for the ufe of the faid Donald Tuo Chambers within the faid Colledge To witt Number Twenty four and Thirtie, with a Sellar for Coalls, and a Garrett in the Steeple for Drying his paper or roumes alfe convenient for the faid ufe ffor the which caufes The faid Donald Govan Binds and obleidges himfelf To furnifh and keep up for the faid fpace of Seven years and Longer during the continuance of his priviledge Tuo preffes for printing with all neceffary Materialls for printing Latin, Greek, Hebrew and Chaldee Att leaſt sua many of Hebrew and Chaldee as are needfull to Print a Small Grammar And Binds and obleidges him to keep fufficient and fkillfull Correctors and Workmen to ferve in the printing houfe And to preferr every member of the Univerſitie to the ufe att leaſt of one prefs to any other whatfoever And to ferve them att the Common rate according to the feveral kynds of print And fhall have to ferve that one prefs Three Setters of Letter att leaſt if required And keep fufficient fonts of Englifh, pica, and Small pica Letters as will sett Tuo Sheets of Print in Englifh or Latin And farder Binds and obleidges him to procure a Coppy of each book to the Liberary of the s^d. Univerſitie befor he agree to print it And to furnifh a Coppy of all fuch books he is to print for himfelf for the ufe forfaid And alfo to Print Programs and other Advertifements for the ufe of the Univerſitie to any Member y^r of Gratis, They alwayes furnifhing him Paper for fuch programs or Advertifements And binds and obleidges him to fullfill and perform his part of the haill premifes In manner above wryten Under the pain of One Thoufand merkes Scotts money of penalty in cafe of failzea attour performance Confenting thir prefents be infert and reg^{rat} In the books of Counfell and Seffion or any oy^{rs} competent that Le^{rs} and exce^{tis} of Horning on fix Dayes and Oy^{rs}. needful may pafs hereon In form as effeirs And yrto Conftituts prors In witnefs q.° of thir pn^{ts}. writtin be Hugh Crawfurd wryr in Glafgow Are Sub^{tt}. att Glafgow Day year and place forfaid Befor thefe wittneffes Thomas young and David Holms Servitors to the faid Univerſitie wittneffes also to the Sub^{tion}. of the Marginall Nott Date forf^d.

        Gers : Carmichaell, P. P.   Jo : Stirling Principal.
        Rob : Simson Math. P.   J. Simson SS. T. P.
        Rob : Dick P. P.   Wm. Forbes Prof. of Law.
                      Jo : Johnstoune Med : Profefs.
                      Al : Dunlop G. L. P.
                      And : Rosse Hum. Profefs.
                      Cha : Morthland LL. O. P.
Thomas Young witnefs.   Donald Govane Junr.
David Holms wittnefs.

No. III.

THE UNIVERSITY OF GLASGOW.

THE following information is extracted from a "Memorial concerning the State of the Univerſity of Glaſgow as it was ye 18th of September 1701 when Mr. Stirling was admitted Principal and as it is now in this preſent year 1717."[*]

As to the method of teaching It had been too ordinary to delay beginning to teach the fyſtem of the feveral Sciences that are taught in the philoſophy claſſes till December or January By which means the faid fyſtems could not be perfected in that year to ye great prejudice of the ſtudents. ffor remedy q^r of It was ordained October 1712 that the fyſtem of the feveral Sciences to be taught every year be begun the firſt of November and farther for the better Improvement of the several years wherein philoſophy is taught It was then appointed that the profeſſor who teaches the firſt year not only finiſh his courfe of Logick but likewife that of Ontology and that in the Batchelour year the profeſſor for that year expede his courfe of pneumaticks and Moral philoſophy against the end of that year that fo in the third and laſt year for philoſophy a complete Syſtem of Natural philoſophy may be explained and finiſhed.

Till the beginning of the year 1710 there had for many years been no publick prelections in this Univerſity excepting fome difcourfes by Doctor [Robert] S^t. clare and Mr. Jameſon. But att that time it was Refolved that the principal and feveral oyr profeſſors in their feveral ffaculties ſhould have publick prelections by turns every week after the publick Examinations were over which for the moſt part has been obfervd, befides which its ufual for the profeſſors of Law, Medicine and Orential Languages to have publick leſſons once a week by turns from the beginning of November till ye firſt day of May."

An account of the manner in which several of the Classes were conducted was drawn up by the Professors apparently about the same period. The papers are now printed from the originals preserved among the archives of the University.

The Methode of teaching divinity at prefent in the Univerſitie at Glaſgow.

1. Ther is ane entire fyſteme of divinity explained to the ſtudents each feſſion of the College, which explication is begun uſually the 2d or 3d dyet after the beginning of the feſſion on the 10th day of Octr. and is continued everie tuefday, wednefday, and thurfday till the fyſteme be finiſhed which uſes to be about the middle of June. The compend explained is Johan: Marlij Theol: Comp: Medulla with which the beginners are defired

---

[*] Wodrow MSS. Advocates' Library. Jac. VI. 27.

to read Pictets didactick compend fome parts of which are alfo explained to them in the hall And our Confeffion of faith is collated with Marle's compend as they go along and the differences with their reafons explained and the preference of the propofitions in our Confeffion proved from Scripture and reafon by which means the principal chapters of our confeffion are explained and its doctrine vindicated and the ftudents are taught to obferve in what points the ordinarie fyftemes of divinity differ from it and why ; and the ftudents are alfo examined on what has been explained.

2ly Everie munday is appointed for the ftudents delivering their Lectures, homilies and prefbyterial exercifes which are cenfured by the ftudents after their deliverie.

3ly Everie friday is appointed for the deliverie of ane exegefis by fome ftudent and publick difputes.

4ly Once in a week or two as found convenient Ther is held a meeting for polemick conference In order to which feveral fyftems of divinity are divided among the ftudents to be read and the books of the popifh, focinian and arminian writers &c. are appointed to be read by fome of the elder ftudents judged fitteft for that purpofe by the profeffor who are to give account of their author's opinions with their principles and chief arguments and wherein contrair to the truth are confuted by the profeffor and their objections anfwered and the truth in oppofition to them eftablifhed and the ftudents are defired to propofe their doubts and have them anfwered.

5ly Ther being no publick meeting on Saturday the ftudents are appointed to meet privately for prayer and conference either in one, two or more focieties according to their number And as a great part of their work are to explain some difficult paffage of Scripture propofed in a former meeting by one of their focietie appointed fo to do and required to prefent in writing the explication of it from the beft commentators he can find which when drawn up in form according to the mind of the Societie is delivered to the profeffor to be revized by him and corrected if needfull and then at a convenient time is read publickly and appointed to be recorded in a book. For the better management of which work ther is a portion of Scripture allotted to each Society the difficult paffages of which they are to explain as they ly in order.

The method that I obferve in teaching the Hebrew Chaldee and Syriack Languages is as follows.

I begin with the Hebrew, and for the better teaching of it, I explain to my Scholars Relands Compend of Altingius's Fundamentum Punctationis, and examin them particularly on every part of it and ufually finifh that Grammar in lefs than the fpace of a month. Then I begin the grammar again, and at the fame time prefcribe a fmall portion of the eafieft of the Hiftorical part of the Bible, to be read, interpreted, and analyf'd, and that it may be the eafier done I for fome leffons at the beginning, read, interpret and analyze the text in their hearing, at the fame time fhewing them how to apply the several rules of the Grammar in these exercifes, and of every leffon I exact a particular account from my Scholars. I continue this method for a month longer by wch time the ftudents come to be pretty well founded in the Elements of ye Hebrew tongue, after which I proceed to the pfalter, of which I prefcribe pretty large portions, at every leffon requiring account of the analyfis, as far as the time will allow, and of the pfalter, I ufually read 30 or 40 pfalms the first year.

The beginning of the fecond year I caufe the fame ftudents revife the Grammar, which takes not up ten days, as alfo read fome parts of the prophets, and book of Job. which they continue to do, while I dictat and explain to y^m a fhort compend of a Chaldee Grammar, and before this be done it is ufually the middle of January, when I begin y^m to the analyfis, of the Chaldee text, which they continue to do, till all contain in the bible be finifhed, but when they begin to the analyfis of the Chaldee text, I begin them likewife to the Syriack grammar which is finifhed as foon as the Chaldee, after which till the feffions end they read ye Syriack text and ordinarily expone 8 or ten chapters that year. And with this proficiency all the fcholars I have hitherto had excepting one who read a little Arabick have fatifyd y^mfelves. as for what relates to other parts of Oriental Learning I have hitherto made little progrefs in teaching of it.

Once in a fortnight I have a publick Leffon upon points abfolutly neceffary to be known by any that defign to improve in that Learning, if conveniency of others permitt I defign to be more frequent for the future.

As for the Students of philofophy, the dyets being fo fhort and the meetings fo few in a year, all I can gett done with them is to Initiat y^m in the Heb : Grammar, and read two or three pfalms in a year with y^m.

Ch : Morthland.

Concerning my methode of teaching philofophy.*

As for my own way of teaching, it is the fame old way y^t I was taught myfelf, and has bin long in ufe in this College; by dited notes, and difputs in all the parts of philofophy; tho' in the logick year, I began always the logicks by teaching thofe of Burgerfdick for two months or fo; and fince the fixing of the bajan Claffe I ufed to take up much time in the beginning of the femie year by caufing thofe y^t were come up to revife y^r Greek, y^t I might both bring it to y^r remembrance and know the ability of every one of y^m y^t way: neither could I well begin y^m w^t the logicks till they were tolerably well gathered : I have caufed y^m to difput q^n they were ready for it fometimes three days in the week, and fometimes more : alfo to get y^r leffons by heart, and be able to give an account of y^m q^ch was chiefly done in the morning; fome time being allowed for difput and fome time for writing, q̃ther in the morning or forenoon as occafion offerd. in the afternoon, efpecially in the end of the year, I have bin in ufe to teach y^m fomething of arithmetick and geometry in the way of dictats : I have alfo caufed y^m to have fometimes exegefes in the Claffe, but not every year, nor yet always in every courfe, finding y^r performances

---

* The first part of this paper contains Remarks on proposed Improvements in conducting the Philosoph Classes, which are not inserted.

but very weak fometimes : but the difputs I never fuffer'd to be neglected, q^{ch} feemed to be the equivalent. this is the fubftance, and I cannot well enlarge. onely my opinion is y^t difputs and dictats muft be kept up as ufually till we fee farder about us : reformations cannot be fudden in thefe cafes, but muft go on by flow degrees, till we can fay y^t the remedie is at leaft better y^n the difeafe if any be.

Jo : LAW.

Method of teaching the Bajan Claffe.

I order what ftudents come the firft day, to bring with them, fome Latin Author, againft the next, fuch as Saluft, Quintus Curtius, Cornelius Nepos, or what other profe book I think moft convenient, and which I can finifh in the time I allott for it.

I defire them at the fame time to prepare in a few dayes, ufually againftt the beginning or middle of the Week after, Verneys Greek Grammar, which is the one I think beft. I am oblidged to goe through fome Latin book, both that I may give the Students time to gather, and likewife becaufe I cannot give them fo great leffons in the Grammar, at firft, as will take up the whole Claffe time in examining, nor fo many of them in a day, as we have meetings, without hurrying, and confufing them, in a ftudy perfectly new to them When they have all got their Grammars, I give them a Leffon in it every day, except munday, which leffon I examine betwixt feven and eight ; fpending the reft of the day in turning their Latin author to Englifh, or elfe in having their Latin or Englifh Verfions, which I give them, when I think proper, examined.

When they have learned in the Grammar the Length of the Verbs, which is ufually about the middle of November, I begin it again, and give them a Leffon betwixt Eleven and Twelve, Explaining it more fully, and teaching them fome things, which I make them paffe the firft time ; but I ftill Continue the Mornings Leffon ; fo that after this, all the time that is fpent in Latin, is betwixt Eight and Nine, and in the afternoon.

About the beginning of December, or toward the time of the Publick Examinations, when they have got the length of the Verbs in M$_t$, I caufe them get the Greek Teftament, in which I give them a Leffon every day betwixt eight and nine. If there be any of the Latin book unexamined, I take it either in the afternoons, or, (in time of the Examination) att what time I can fpare in the other Dyets, becaufe I always endeavour to have it ended againft the beginning of January. About which time, having ended the Verbs in M$_t$, they get some eafy profe Greek book, fuch as Cebes' Table, Æfops ffables, Lucian's Dialogues or his Timon, which they learn five times a week betwixt Eight and Nine, taking the Leffon they had at that hour in the Teftament, betwixt Eleven and Twelve, and That in the Grammar the afternoon, which laft Leffon I continue all the year, at leaft till they have gone through the Grammar wholly in the Morning Leffon.

When they come to the fyntax, which may be about the middle of ffebruary, I give them fome harder book fuch as Xenophon's Cyropædia, Herodian, Ifocrates, Ariftophanes though a Poet, in which they have their morning leffon, and if there remain any of the former book untaught, I teach it in the forenoon, in which cafe, I give no more Leffons in the Teſtament, except a ſhort one, on Mondays before nine; but if the other book before mentioned be Ended, I then continue the forenoons Leſſon in the Teſtament, till they begin a Poet.

When the ſyntax is ended, I begin immediately to teach the Dialects, before I teach what is betwixt, that I may the ſooner fit them for reading the Poets, which when they have gone through, I give them ſome Poet, uſually Homers Iliad, which they give ane account of in the morning, turning the laſt mentioned Book to the forenoon. This I continue all year, only now and then, after they have learned the Syntax, I give them ſome Latin ſentences to Tranſlate to Greek, and ſometimes ſome Greek Paſſages, which I know they have not a verſion of, to render in Latin.

When they have gone through the whole Grammar in the Morning's leſſon, I either take what remains of it in the Afternoons Leſſon, or elſe I teach Homer all the Morning. If I doe the firſt, then in the afternoon I either goe through Some part of the Grammar, for the third time, if I think it neceſſary, or elſe I teach them in the afternoon the ſame book they have in the forenoon.

AL : DUNLOP.

The "Statute and Act regulating the Univerſity of Glaſgow," mentioned at page 11 of this work, was drawn up by the Committee of Visitation, and is dated 19th September, 1727. The extracts here printed, as confirming the statements there made, are taken from a copy preserved in the General Register House.

"And the Commiſſion having recommended to the Maſters of the ſaids three philoſophy Claſſes to make their election which of the Claſſes they were ſeverally to take And they having agreeed among themſelves And Mr. Gerſham Carmichael having made choiſe of the Ethick Claſs, Mr. John Loudoun of the Logick Claſs, and the teaching of the Phyſick Claſs falling to Mr. Robert Dick,

The Commiſſioners Statute and Ordain That the ſaids perſons reſpective have in time coming the teaching of the ſaid ſeverall Claſſes by them choſen And that Mr. Robert Dick teach the Claſs falling to him, And that they remain ſo fixed to the ſaid Claſſes, and that all other and ſubſequent profeſſors of philoſophy coming in to the ſaid Univerſity be ſtill fixed to one claſs, and the teaching of the forſaid particular parts of philoſophy allotted to the Claſs in which he ſhall be fixt.

That the profeſſors of Divinity, Law, Medicine, Orientall Languages, Mathematicks and Hiſtory Shall yearly teach the buſineſs of their reſpective profeſſions whenever five or more Schollars ſhall apply to them, and that they give not under four leſſons every week.

That in caſe the ſaid number of Five Schollars do not apply to the ſaid profeſſors betwixt the ſitting down of the Colledge and the firſt day of December thereafter, That ſuch profeſſor ſhall after the firſt day of December aforſaid Prelect publickly once every week at ſuch hour and upon ſuch day of the week as the faculty ſhall appoint.

That the Profeſſors above ſpecified ſhall either continue their Colleges from the firſt day of November to the laſt day of May yearly, or if their Claſſes be ſooner finiſhed

That they fhall weekly thereafter give publick preleċtions to the laſt day of May as in the cafe of Scholars not applying for teaching.

That the Profeffor of Bottony and Anatomy* teach Bottony yearly from the fifteenth day of May to the firſt day of July, if five fchollars offerr.

And finds and Declares That Dr. Brifbane prefent profeffor of Bottony and Anatomy in the faid Univerfity is obliged to teach Anatomy as well as Bottony, And ordains him to teach Anatomy yearly as the other profeffors abovementioned are appointed to teach the bufinefs of their profeffions, and that he begin to teach fo foon as ten fchollars offerr, and if no fuch number offerr before the firſt day of November That thereafter he fhall preleċt publickly on Anatomy once every week as other profeffors are to doe in the like cafe untill the fifteenth day of May that he begin to teach Bottany.

No. IV.

DR JAMES MOOR.

JAMES MOOR, professor of Greek in the University of Glasgow, was the son of James Muir, school-master in Glasgow, and considered himself descended from Elizabeth Mure, the queen of Robert II., from whom he had constructed a genealogical table of his ancestors. His father appears to have been a man of considerable learning, and of such unwearied industry, that we are told, "that not thinking himself rich enough to buy Newton's Principia, he copied the whole of it with his own hand." He died while his son was very young, and his widow sold his library,—a circumstance which Dr Moor often regretted.

After acquiring the usual preliminary branches of education, Moor entered the University as a student of Humanity in 1725, and his studies were greatly facilitated by his acquaintance with Mr Andrew Stalker, who has been already noticed in this work (pp. 7—9), and who kindly allowed him to read in his shop as much as he pleased, "which permission," says our authority, "he made much use of." Of his progress while at College we have the most flattering proofs. The Natural Philosophy Class was at this time taught by Mr Robert Dick, (See No. III.). and the Professor, after demonstrating a proposition to his students, used to desire Moor to go over it a second time, instead of doing it himself. He was particularly fond of the Mathematics, and had from an early period attained to such proficiency in that science, that his degree of Master of Arts, instead of testifying in the usual form that he had made *progressus haud spernendos*, bore upon it *progressus egregios*. But while engaged in these pursuits he had neglected the Greek

---

* Anatomy and Botany were at this time, and till lately, taught by the same Professor.

language, and on resuming it found he had almost entirely forgot it. From this circumstance, he used to recommend to those who wished to retain their knowledge of the languages, to allot a small portion of each day to them while engaged in other studies.

It cannot be ascertained at what precise period Moor took his degree, as the Laureation Book has been unfortunately mislaid, but it must have been between this period and 1743. After leaving the University he seems to have kept a school in Glasgow, in which he taught several branches of education. While thus employed he read the classics at his leisure hours.

He was next employed as tutor to the Earls of Errol and Selkirk, in which capacity he travelled abroad. He was afterwards in the family of the Earl of Kilmarnock. When in the last situation he had made a collection of books which he valued highly, but unfortunately while the Earl was from home, the family mansion, along with Moor's library, was burned. At this period he studied much,—principally late in the evening, and prevented himself from becoming drowsy by drinking strong tea. His health was thus considerably impaired, and he "had at times some severe fevers." As a tutor he was diligent and attentive to his pupils. The son of the Earl of Kilmarnock especially made such proficiency, that he taught him Greek without his father's knowledge, until he read before him by his tutor's desire an ode of Anacreon, "to the great surprize and joy of the earl." He also mentions in the Dedication of his Essays, that the Earl of Errol had, "at a very early time of life, made, in that language, a very uncommon progress."

On the 11th November, 1742, Mr. Moor was appointed Librarian to the University, in the place of Mr Dunlop (probably the subsequent Professor of Oriental Languages), and in May, 1743, the appointment was continued by the Town Council for four years "from the end of the year for which he was chosen by the College." It may be necessary to mention, that at this time the right of presentation to this office was vested alternately in the Magistrates and Town Council and in the College, and that each presentation was considered as lasting for four years.

He had remained in this situation for about three years, when Mr Alexander Dunlop, who had been Professor of Greek for more than forty years, and whose sight was now considerably decayed, resigned his chair upon condition that his salary should be continued during his life, and that he should still possess the house in which he had lived, "under the same regulations and conditions as the other Masters possess their houses."* Moor

---

* Mr. Dunlop did not survive hi resignation long. His death is thus noticed in the Glasgow Journal:—"April 27, 1747. On Friday last died, universally lamented, Mr. Alex. Dunlop, late Professor of Greek in the University of Glasgow, which office he held upwards of 40 years with general applause. His thorough knowledge and fine taste in that language, with his masterly and engaging method of teaching it, raised the study thereof, which had been long neglected, unto general esteem and reputation. His true piety, solid judgment, and cheerfulness of temper, which continued to the last, though labouring for some time under a disease he knew to be mortal, added to the many other excellent qualifications he was possessed of, made him a most useful member of society, and an ornament to his profession." Professor Dunlop was the son of Principal Dunlop of Glasgow, and brother to the celebrated William Dunlop, Professor of Divinity in the University of Edinburgh.

was elected his successor on the 9th of July following, and had a Critical Explication of the tenth chapter of Longinus assigned to him as a Trial Discourse. For this situation, his son mentions that Moor paid Dunlop £600, which was advanced by the Earl of Selkirk.

The Rebellion had been terminated but a few months before by the battle of Culloden, and although its effects, so far as concerned Moor's professional labours, might be considered as at an end, he was now called upon to mourn the loss of his generous patron, the Earl of Kilmarnock. That unfortunate nobleman, it will be recollected, had taken an active part on the side of the Chevalier, and for this offence he was condemned and executed. At the request of his lordship's relations, Moor went to London to solicit the ministers on his behalf. He had not imbibed the political sentiments of his patron, and his marked attachment to the reigning family, perhaps, rendered it possible that his intercession might be the means of procuring his pardon. In this, however, he was unsuccessful.

In 1747 Mr Moor ceased to be librarian, his term of four years having expired, and from that time he was wholly occupied in classical pursuits. Of his success we have the best proofs in the works on Greek literature which he produced.

We have already noticed (p. 30) the splendid folio edition of Homer, which was edited by professors Moor and Muirhead at the request of the University; and his son mentions that "he inspected an edition of Herodotus, and, it is thought, some more of the classics of Foulis." His Greek Grammar, which he left incomplete, has long been considered as a standard work; "and in it," says Dr Irving, "we meet with instances of a beautiful analysis." He was one of the twelve constituent members of the Literary Society of Glasgow, and the only other printed works which bear his name are the results of his connection with that Society,—of these, and his other Essays read to that Institution, a list is given at the end of this article. His partiality to books,—of which he had formed a large collection, has been formerly adverted to. Besides this, he selected a cabinet of medals, which the University purchased in November, 1769. His library was bought by Mr James Spotiswood, whose name has been mentioned as having become the possessor of Foulis's stock of books, and was exposed to Sale in February, 1779. The catalogue (which is entitled "Bibliotheca Mooriana") contains 2724 articles, in every department of literature, more particularly Grecian, and Mathematical science.

In 1761 Moor was appointed Vice-Rector by the Earl of Errol, then Lord Rector; and in April, 1763, he applied for the degree of Doctor of Laws, which was granted him by the University, in consideration of his talents and services. Three years afterwards he was appointed Clerk to the University, but his health was now so much broken, that he requested and obtained leave to employ an assistant in teaching his public and private classes, in case of his own inability. He regained his strength considerably, but for the last twelve years of his life he seems to have enjoyed little good health,—a circumstance which inflamed a temper naturally irritable. In March, 1774, he found himself so much exhausted, that he offered to resign his professorship, if the Faculty would appoint Mr John Young (who had been his assistant) successor, but to this they would not consent.

Accordingly, on the 5th of May, he subscribed a deed of resignation, on condition that he should be allowed to retain his house and salary, which his colleagues accepted.

Of the remaining part of his life little is known. His death, which took place on September, 17th, 1779, is thus noticed in the newspapers of the day :—"On Friday the 17th current, died here, James Moor, LL.D. Emeritus Profeſſor of Greek in the Univerſity of Glaſgow, eminent for his learning, of which he has left a lasting monument in his writings, particularly in his excellent Grammar of the Greek Language; and no leſs eminent for his affectionate goodneſs of heart, of which he has left a faithful remembrance in the breaſts of his friends." When a child, Moor lost the sight of one of his eyes in the measles. His constitution was naturally weakly, and was probably rendered more so from the exertions which he made in the acquisition of knowledge. This, perhaps, added to his irritability of temper, and led to some unseemly exhibitions of violence in his class.

Of Moor's talents as a philologist, no doubt can be entertained; but some of his other literary productions are beneath criticism. He wrote several odes, one of which, entitled "The Linnet, or Happiness at Home," appeared in Dr Gilbert Stuart's series of the Edinburgh Review and Magazine, in November, 1775. Unfortunately the Doctor's housekeeper makes a conspicuous figure on this, as on too many other occasions. But perhaps the most curious of Moor's poetical productions is his Epitaph, written by himself, and which we are now enabled to print from a copy in Mr David Laing's possession.

To MR. P. R. [PROFESSOR RICHARDSON?]

I have a thing done my dear Willy,
Which well conſidered is not ſilly;
I have,—but promiſe ye wont laugh,
I have wrote mine own Epitaph.
From vanity ye will not free it.
Nor ſhould, I grant;—yet come and ſee it.
You'll find I do the beſt I can,
To imitate my ſiſter Swan;
And ſtep out of the world in June—
Step which I judge I may ſtep ſoon.
  Valete ſtep plumbline deorſum
  Sad *supine* ſtep upon the *Dorsum*.

EPITAPH.

Here lye the Bones of D[octor Moor]
Who lived contented tho' but poor
Piece of a poet he was once
By Inſpiration or by Chance.

> Nor was he very far to feek
> Either in Latin or in Greek.
> Moreover too,—which is no low matter—
> He was well verf'd in Greek Geometry :*
> Knew too the Rules and the Reductions
> Of Algebra, Fluents and Fluxions.
> Could penetrate into the natures
> Of Curves, their Tangencies and Quadratures,
> And bring to fluxional Equation
> Problems of Curve—Rectification ;
> Friend of the fatherlefs and poor
> Who weep† the Death of D[octor Moor]
> Know that thefe verfes, ye who fee 'em
> Were by himfelf wrote—ante diem.
> "Himfelf too much he praifes"—"Hufh!
> Or ye will make his afhes blufh.
> Had he himfelf not done it, Brother!
> It ne'er had been done by another."

This Epitaph was copied from the original in the hand writing of Dr Moor by the Rev. Dr Traill (the biographer of Dr Robert Simson), who procured it, with a few others of Moor's papers, from the late Andrew Foulis. The other notices are taken from a short memoir drawn up by Moor's son, and from the University Records.

ESSAYS READ BY DR MOOR IN THE LITERARY SOCIETY.

February 6, 1752. An Effay on Hiftorical Compofition.
This was the first Essay read in the Literary Society. See No. V.
March 1, 1754. An Effay on the Compofition of the Picture defcribed in the Dialogue of Cebes.
February 8, 1755. An Effay on the Influence of Philosophy upon the Fine Arts.
On the End of Tragedy according to Ariftotle.
First published in 1763.
November 30, 1764. On the Structure of the Greek Language, and the Method of ascertaining the meaning of the Particles of that Tongue.
November 29, 1765. Remarks on Dr. Warburton's Critical Notes on Mr. Pope, in his laft edition of his Works.
An Effay on the Prepofitions of the Greek Language. 1766.
December 9, 1769. Some Obfervations on the Genius of Englifh Verfe.

---

* Perhaps these lines should be read thus,
    Moreover too,—which is no low matter,—he
    Was well vers'd in Greek Geometry.

† In the MS. the word "wail" is written above as an amendment.

No. V.

THE LITERARY SOCIETY OF GLASGOW.

SINCE the notice of the Literary Society, at page 15, was printed, the following Extracts from the first volume of the Records have been received. They are in the hand-writing of Professor Richardson.

"Friday, January 10th, 1752. It was agreed at this firft meeting of the firft twelve members of the Literary Society in Glafgow College, that they fhould meet weekly on Thurfday at half an hour after fix o'clock afternoon; And that one of the fociety fhould read a Paper drawn up by him, which might be the fubject of converfation at that meeting. And the members having by lot drawn the numbers as in the lift adjoining, it was agreed that no difcourfe fhould be read before February 6th or 7th; but that at the three firft meetings, fome of the fociety fhould read an account of fome new book. It was also agreed, that at that, and the fucceeding meeting, a Prefes fhould be chofen, And that thereafter, the member who read to the Society fhould be the Prefident of the next meeting; and that the Prefident immediately after the difcourfe was read, fhould afk the members prefent their opinions and what they had to fay on the fubject of the difcourfe."

The twelve constituent members were,

Mr. James Moor, Prof^r. of Greek.
Dr. Robert Hamilton, Prof^r. of Anatomy.
Dr. [William] Leechman, Prof^r. of Divinity.
Mr. James Clow, Prof^r. of Logic.
Mr. Hercules Lindfay, Prof^r. of Law.
Dr. Robert Dick, Prof^r. of Nat. Philofophy.

Rev. Mr. William Craig, Min^r. of Glafgow.
Mr. George Rofs, Prof^r. of Humanity.
Dr. William Cullen, Prof^r. of Medicine.
Mr. Adam Smith, Prof^r. of Moral Philofophy.
Mr. Richard Betham.
Dr. John Brifbane.

Though the above were the constituent members, the following were also considered as members, and joined at the ensuing meetings.

Mr. William Ruat, Prof^r. of Church Hiftory.
Mr. Robert Bogle, merchant in Glafgow.
Mr. Alexander Graham.
Mr. William Crawford, merchant in Glafgow.
Mr. George Maxwell.
Dr. Robert Simfon, Prof^r. of Mathematics.

John Dalrymple, Efq. Advocate, (now Sir John Dalrymple).
William Mure of Caldwell, Efq.
The Rev^d. and Honble. Pat: Boyle.
Walter Stuart, Efq. Advocate.
Mr. Thomas Melville.

Extracted from the minutes of some of the ensuing meetings :—

Jany. 16. Dr. Cullen read an account of a treatife entitled Cofmologie by Maupertuis.—
Jany. 23. Mr. Smith read an Account of fome of Mr. David Hume's Effays on Commerce.—

Jany. 30. Mr. Clow read an account of Harris's Hermes. It was then agreed to change the day of meeting to Friday: and on Friday Feby. 7. Mr. Moor read the firſt difcourfe entitled "On Hiſtorical Compoſition."

In 1753 the Society received the following additional members:—

John Graham, Eſq. of Dougaldſton.
John Callender, Eſq. of Craigforth.
David Hume, Eſq.
Mr. George Moorhead, afterwards Prof^r. of Humanity.
Mr. Robert Foulis, Univerſity Printer.*

Mr. John Anderſon, afterwards Prof^r. of Nat: Philoſophy.
Mr. Ferguſon, now I believe in Edinburgh College.
Mr. Wait.

In 1756—57, and afterwards,

Mr. Andrew Foulis, Printer.
Mr. William Campbell.
Mr. Alexander Wilſon, Prof^r of Aſtronomy.
Dr. Joſeph Black, Prof^r. of Medicine.
Mr. Andrews.

Dr. Alexander Stevenſon, afterwards Prof^r. of Medicine.
Rev^d. Mr. Mackay.
Mr. Thomas Hamilton, Prof^r. of Anatomy.
Mr. James Buchanan, Prof^r. of Hebrew.
Rev^d. Mr. James Crombie.

In 1761.

Mr. John Millar, Prof^r. of Law.
Dr. Trail, Prof^r of Divinity.

Mr. Cumin, Prof^r. of Hebrew.
Dr. Williamſon, Prof^r. of Mathematics.

In 1762—63.

Dr. Wight, Prof^r. of Church Hiſtory.
Mr. Ogilvie, now I believe a Prof^r. in Aberdeen.

George Oſwald, Eſq. [of Scotſtown].
Lord Cardroſs, now Earl of Buchan.

In 1764, and afterwards,

Dr. Walker, Miniſter of Moffat.
Dr. Thomas Reid, Prof^r. of Moral Philoſophy.

Mr. Robinſon, now in Edinburgh College.
Dr. Irvine, Lecturer on Chemiſtry

In 1773—1774, and afterwards,

Mr. W^m. Richardſon, Prof^r. of Humanity.
Mr. Geo: Jardine, Prof^r. of Logic.
Mr. John Young, Prof^r. of Greek.
Mr. Arch^d. Arthur, Prof^r. of Moral Philoſophy.

Rev^d. Mr. James Bell, College-Chaplain, afterwards Min^r. of Coldſtream.
Dr. Taylor, now Miniſter of Glaſgow.
Mr. John Wright, a miniſter in Perthſhire, then a College-Chaplain.

---

* Mr. Foulis was therefore not an original member, as stated at page 15, on the authority of Richardson's Letter.

Wᵐ. Craig, Advocate [now Lord Craig].
Revᵈ. Dr. Charters, Minʳ. of Wilton.
Mr. Gilbert Hamilton, Merchant in Glafgow.
Mr. Archᵈ. Graham, merchant in Glafgow, [afterwards Cashier of the Thistle Bank].
Dr. Bailie, Profʳ. of Divinity.
Dr. Walter Young, Minʳ. of Erfkine.
Dr. Finlay, Profʳ. of Divinity.
Revᵈ. Mr. Hugh M'Diarmid.
Revᵈ. Mr. Andrew M'Donald.
Dr. Davidfon, Principal of the Univerfity.
Mr. Wᵐ. Hamilton, Profʳ. of Anatomy.
Dr. Taylor, then Minifter, now Principal of the Univerfity.
Dr. Couper, now Profʳ. of Aftronomy.
Dr. Richard Millar, Lecturer on Materia Medica.
Dr. Cleghorn, Lecturer on Chemiftry.
Dr. M'Leod, Profʳ. of [Church] Hiftory.

Mr. Mylne, now Profʳ. of Moral Philofophy.
Dr. Pat : Graham, Minʳ. of Aberfoyle.
Mr. John Millar, Advocate.
Dr. John Lockhart, Minʳ. in Glafgow.
Dr. Hope, Profʳ. [of Chemistry] in Edinburgh.
Dr. James Jeffray, Profʳ. of Anatomy.
Mr. James Millar, Profʳ. of Mathematics.
Dr. J. Brown, now living at St. Andrews.
Dr. Thomas Brown, lecturer on Botany.
Mr. Macturk, Affiftant Profʳ. of [Church] Hiftory.
Mr. Alexʳ. Craig.
Dr. Carmichael.
Dr. Marfhal.
Mr. Pat : Wilfon, afterwards Profʳ. of Aftronomy.
Mr. Dunlop, Surgeon in Glafgow.

In 1787, and afterwards,

Revᵈ. Dr. Rankin, Minʳ. in Glafgow.
Mr. Finlay of Bogfide.
Dr. Freer, Profʳ. of Medicine.
Mr. Robert Davidfon, Profʳ. of Law.
Revᵈ. Dr. Macgill, Minʳ. in Glafgow.
Mr. Jackfon, at Ayr.
Dr. Meikleham, Profʳ. of Nat : Philofophy.

The Revᵈ. Mr. Gavin Gibb, Minifter of Strathblane, [afterwards Minʳ. of St. Andrews Church, and Profʳ. of Oriental Languages].
Mr. Lockhart Moorhead, Librarian to the Univerfity, [afterwards Profʳ. of Nat : History].

ESSAYS READ BEFORE THE SOCIETY BY ROBERT FOULIS.*

Novʳ. 9. 1764. Memoir on the Difcovery and Culture of Genius.
March. 29. 1765. What is Faction diftinguifhed from Patriotifm.
Novʳ. 8. 1765. A Difcourfe concerning the Animofities between England and Scotland.
Novʳ. 14. 1766. Obfervations on the Knowledge or Science neceffary to a Commercial Town or State.
Febʸ. 27. 1767. Whether a general Convention of Deputies from the different princes of Europe in order to find out what might be for the public good of their refpective States might not conduce to the good of the whole.

---

* These lists also include the questions proposed by the brothers.

Nov[r.] 13. 1767. Some farther Illustrations of the advantages which might arise from an annual Convention represeting the different States of Europe.

Dec[r.] 4. 1767. From what reasons founded in nature do the Imitative Arts of Music, Painting, and Poetry proceed.

March. 11. 1768. Whether is it true that those who with a good education would make the best men with a bad one make the worst.

Nov[r.] 18. 1768. An account of the Chevalier Ramsay's Principles of Universal Religion.

March. 17. 1769. What is the connection between things human and divine hinted at by M. Antoninus in Par. 13. Book 3. and wherein lies the importance of attending to this connection in [order to] our performing aright every duty we owe to God or man.

Nov[r.] 10 1769. On the establishments wanting in this University which are necessary to render education more complete.

Feb[y.] 24. 1770. Whether Learning, Arts, Sciences and Manners in Europe are upon the whole on the Advance or Decline.

May 4. 1770. What would be the probable consequence of departing from the present law with regard to Literary Property and making that property perpetual.

Nov[r.] 9. 1770. Continuation of the Subject Literary Property.

Nov[r.] 8. 1771. On the improvement of Agriculture and at the same time diminishing the expence.

Essays Read by Andrew Foulis.

Dec. 14. 1764. On the first Religion of Mankind and the notion of a chaos.

Dec. 13. 1765. On the Advancement of Learning.

Mar. 7. 1766. Whether a stricter Police with regard to Morals might not be established in Britain consistent with Liberty.

Dec. 9. 1766. A Discourse concerning Literary Property.

March. 13. 1767. Wherein lyes the superior excellence of the Virtue of Simplicity.

Dec. 18. 1667. Some Reflections on National Prosperity, particularly that of Great Britain.

Mar. 25. 1768. Would it be for the benefit of the public to diminish the number of Capital Punishments.

Dec. 23. 1768. Reflexions on the degree of Compassion due to follies and vices of mankind.

April 28. 1769. In order to an equal representation of Property and People ought not the power to be taken from decayed Burghs and given to those which have increased.

Dec. 15. 1769. Some Account of the Egyptian Papyrus and other materials which the Ancients used to write upon.

Dec. 21. 1770. An Account of some great Libraries among the Ancients.

No. VI.

ROBERT FOULIS'S LAST LETTER TO HIS PARTNERS.

MESSRS GLASSFORD, CAMPBELL, AND INGRAM,

GENTLEMEN,
                                                                               LONDON, *April 29th,* 1776.

BEFORE your letter came to hand, the time came on that it became neceffary to confult and decide what was to be done with refpect to a Sale this year. Mr. Ingram and Mr. Gordon (fortunately coming to London) went along with me to Mr. Chriftie, to have his judgment how and when we should proceed. Mr. Chriftie is undoubtedly the moft knowing judge in Britain being ftored with knowledge arifing from daily experience, as the chief Sales are made by him. The employment of no particular Sale can be a great object to him, becaufe he has always more in his offer than he can accept: his intereft being the fame with the proprietor of the Pictures, as the fuccefs not only increafes his commiffion, but supports his reputation, which is of great importance to him becaufe it throws all the bufinefs of London into his hands. Having met with this gentleman and he being before apprifed that the gentlemen who waited on him had a joint intereft in the pictures, he fpoke to the following purpofe; Gentlemen, When Mr. Foulis firft came to Town, I made a propofal to him of felecting a number of his Pictures to intermix with a Sale which I had in view; Mr. Foulis feemed willing to accept of this propofal, but it was over-ruled, and the only opportunity I had of ferving him this feafon loft; for a Sale on the days propofed would have had no company, and you run the hazard of being offered half-a-crown for what you expect 20 pounds. This difeafe of a glutted market has been gradually brought on thefe ten years paft by five or fix people yearly importing new collections, and has been brought to a crifis by thefe importations, and by an. Englifhman who had gone to Paris and eftablifhed a Paper Manufactory there for lining walls: This man had fallen into the commerce of Pictures, and engaged a number of wealthy people at Paris to lay out their money in that way, and accordingly a great collection of paintings was brought into London, and an unfuccefful Sale attempted, in which the perfons concerned bought in the Pictures, and he underftood that the whole would be recalled back to Paris, where their higheft priced Pictures had generally gone, being bought by Frenchmen who came to London for that purpofe and commonly in prefence of many of the Englifh Nobility; And Mr. Chriftie gave feveral inftances, particularly of the gentleman who bought Crawford Moor from Lord Selkirk, and other examples more recent; and faid that this difeafe being brought to a crifis would prove its own cure, for to his certain knowledge none of the perfons who ufed to import any Pictures annually would go abroad this year, they having all fuffered feverely for what they had done; and he thought that in confequence next meeting of Parliament muft afford a better market for Pictures than any that had been for feveral years paft, fo that attempting a Sale in the prefent indifpofition of the public, would be attempting a thing impracticable and deftructive beyond meafure. Thefe and the like reafons fatisfied Mr. Gordon and Mr. Ingram, that a Sale fhould not be attempted this year. Altho' this was a profound humiliation to me, having undertaken this with fanguine hopes of fuccefs, and fo much the more afflicting as I fee fuch a defponding fpirit, which in reality there is no good reafon for, becaufe the collection is upon the whole undoubtedly the beft ever offered to Sale in London, never any containing fo many capital pictures of the leading Mafters of every School. I have, indeed, been greatly difappointed in my expectations of drawing the attention of the public; the advertifements are fo innumerable, and the papers themfelves fo numerous that the expence becomes great, and the progrefs in making any thing known to the public aftonifhingly flow. None of the principal Exhibitions lay out lefs than 300 pounds in advertifing, and a like fum upon Catalogues which they give away; and this year there have been Exhibitions in all quarters, and above 40 or 50 different kinds. The vifits that I have had, have been generally promifing to bring fomething good at laft, becaufe they have been perfons of rank, perfons who have been in Italy and feen the beft collections there; and fome moft knowing gentlemen left this teftimony that they never had feen any collection that bore fo many genuine marks of originality. I have illuftrated the principal pictures to almoft every perfon who feemed to deferve it; more particularly the Transfiguration, becaufe I apprehend there was fomething fo wonderful in falling upon that, that I did not expect to make the tenth part of the progrefs I have made in eftablifhing its reputation; and were it generally known to princes to be what it really is, fo as to raife competition for obtaining it, it ought in courfe to give a greater price than any Picture has given fince the Reftoration of Painting; becaufe the Roman Picture is efteemed the moft valuable in the world, and altho' larger, yet in many refpects left imperfect in comparifon of this, which I have endeavoured to fhew in detail every day to the moft inquifitive.

I am forry for the expence that has been incurred: were it in my power the Company fhould fee my gratitude. The care of the Pictures has been no eafy matter; they have furnifhed perpetual occupation, but not without doing them good. What further particulars may be thought proper I beg Mr. John Ingram to add, after taking the trouble of reading this letter. You have exercifed much patience in the whole of this affair, exert prudence and magnanimity to the laft, and truft that God will fend you his Bleffing,

I am, with my beft wifhes to you all
your moft faithful
and ob^t. Servant
ROBERT FOULIS.

No. VII.

PAPER USED BY ROBERT AND ANDREW FOULIS.

The following curious statement, from the papers of Mr John Fleming, has been communicated by the Reverend Dr Fleming, Professor of Oriental Languages in the University of Glasgow. Unfortunately it came too late to be referred to in the Account of Printing.

A Lift of all the Paper made ufe of in printing Greek and Lat. Claffics from the year 1742 to 1765 by Messrs. R. & A. Foulis, with the Drawback on the same.

			s.	d.		£	s.	d.
3148	Reams, 11	quires of fine Foolfcap	1	0		157	8	6
73	Ditto, 10	qurs. — Second Do.	0	9		2	15	1½
902	Ditto, 16½	qurs. — Fine Pot	1	0		45	2	9
461	Ditto, 11	qurs. — Second Do.	0	6	per Ream	10	10	9
131	Ditto, 7	qurs. — Fine Crown	1	0		6	11	5
145	Ditto, 12	qurs. — Fine Demy	1	6		10	18	6
97	Ditto, 17	qurs. — Second Do.	1	0		4	17	11
22	Ditto, Treafury Poft		1	6		1	13	0

£239 17 11½

By an Act of the 10th Q. Anne the above Drawbacks were granted upon paper made in Gr. Britain, providing that the sd. paper be ufed in printing any books in ye Latin, Greek, Oriental, or Northern languages within the Univerfities of Scotland, or any of them by permiffion of the Principal for 32 years from 1712.

By Act of ye 12th Q. Anne, the following additional Duties upon paper made in Britain, and with the like difcount and drawbacks, as in ye former Act, for 32 years, from 1714, viz.

                                                                                     d.

Demy fine 9
Demy fecond 6
Crown fine 6
Crown fecond 4½
Foolfcap fine 6
Ditto fecond .... 4½   per Ream.
Fine Pot 6
Second Pot 3
Brown large cap............................ 3
Small ordinary brown 2

The Duties and Drawback in ye 1st. Act are made perpetual by Act in ye 3d year, George 1st.

The Duties and Drawback in ye other Act are made perpetual by Act 6th. Geo. 1st.

INDEX.

ABERDEEN, 6, 82.
Adams, James, 25.
Alberti, 22.
Allan, David, 88, 90.
Anderson, Andrew, 2, 3.
—————————— his heirs, 3.
—————— George, 1, 14, 120.
—————— John, Dumbarton, 4.
—————— Professor John, 133.
Andrews, Mr, 133.
Angelo, Michael, 43.
Arbuthnot, Mr, 33.
Arthur, Professor, 15, 16, 133.
Argyle, Duke of, 20, 27, 86.
Auldhouse, Robert Sanders of, 3.
Ayr, 6.

Baillie, Dr James, 134.
Baird, Miss Jenny, 9.
—————— Miss Mally, 9.
Beattie, Dr James, 32, 33, 34, 36.
Bell, Rev. James, 133.
Betham, Richard, 132.
Black, Dr Joseph, 16, 25, 28, 43, 133.
Blaeu, his Atlas, 82.
Bogle, Robert, 132.
Boyle, Patrick, 132.
Boutcher, Miss, 43.
—————— William, 43.
Brechin, 6.
Brisbane, Dr, 127.

Brisbane, Dr John, 132.
Brown, Dr J., 134.
—————— Dr Thomas, 134.
Buchan, Earl of, 23, 133.
Buchanan, Professor James, 133.
—————— William, 87.
Bute, Earl of, 90.

Callender, John, of Craigforth, 133.
Camlachie, village of, 13.
Campbell, John, of Clathic, 18, 38.
—————— of Shawfield, 88.
—————— William, 133.
Capperonier, M., 22.
Cardross, Lord [Earl of Buchan], 133.
Carmichael, Gersham, 120, 121, 126.
—————— Dr, 134.
Chalmers, Sir George, 81.
Chapman, Robert, 46.
Charles the First, 1, 81.
—————— the Second, 10.
Charteris, Rev. Dr, 133.
Christie, Mr, 136.
Clark, Dr Samuel, 15, 31.
Cleghorn, Dr Robert, 134.
Clow, Professor, 15, 132, 133.
Cochran, William, 24, 84, 86, 88.
Colquhoun, James, 82.
Cordiner, Charles, 87.
Couper, Dr James, 134.
Coutts, James, 85.

Craig, Alexander, 134.
―― John, 15.
―― Rev. William, 132.
―― William [Lord Craig], 134.
Craufurd, Hugh, 121.
―――― William, 23, 29, 132.
Crombie, Rev. James, 133.
Cullen, Dr, 25, 132.
Culloden, Battle of, 129.
Cumin, Professor, 133.

Dalrymple, Sir John, 23, 28, 132.
Danby, Earl of, 86.
Darien Expedition, 11.
Davidson, Principal, 134.
―――― Professor, 134.
Dennistoun, James, of Colgreine, 9.
Dewar, Robert, 38.
Dibdin, Rev. T. F., 14.
Dick, Robert, 120, 121, 126, 127, 132.
Dodsley, the bookseller, 33, 34.
Douglas, Dr, 40.
Dryden, John, 29.
Dumbarton, 6.
Dumblain, 7.
Dumfries, 6.
Duncan, James, printer, 5.
――――――――― bookseller, 46.
Dundee, 6.
Dunlop, Alexander, 120, 121, 126, 128, 129.
―――― Mr [University Librarian], 128.
―――― Mr, 134.
―――― Principal, 128.
―――― William, 128.

Edinburgh, 1, 2, 4, 16, 29, 30, 31, 40, 43, 46, 82, 84, 85, 128.
Edmonston, Colonel, 88.
Elizabeth, Queen, 85.
Elliot, Mr, 28.
Elzevir, 19, 33, 35.
England, 85.

England, New, 14.
Errol, Earl of, 128, 129.
Etiennes, 33.

Faulls, Andrew, 9.
Fergus the First, 82.
Fergusson, Adam, 25, 133.
Findlay, Dr, 134.
Finlay, Mr, of Bogside, 134.
Flanders, 85.
Fleming, Robert, 83, 84.
Fleming and Yair, 27.
Forbes, William, 120, 121.
Foulis, Andrew [brother of Robert], his birth and education, 10—becomes a member of the Literary Society, and reads discourses there, 16, 133, 135—is dissuaded from the Academy, but afterwards becomes a partner, 19—officiates as auctioneer, 42—dies, 37—his indefatigable industry, 37.
―――― Andrew [son of Robert], 16, 36, 43, 131.
―――― James, 10.
―――― John, 10.
―――― Robert, his birth and parentage, 9—sent apprentice to a barber, 10—attends the University, 10—visits Oxford and the continent, 11—commences bookseller, 12—had several books printed by Urie, 6—commences printer, 12—appointed University printer, 13—first books printed by him, 14—his marriage, 43—his second marriage, 43—elected member of the Literary Society, 15, 133—his essays read there, 16, 134, 135—the Academy is instituted, 18—his motives for it, 17, 82—is dissuaded from it by Mr Townshend and others, 19—his letter to Harvock, 20, 21, 22—his difficulty in procuring teachers, 84—Sir John Dalrymple's letter to him, 23—28—becomes acquainted with Pro-

fessor Richardson, 31—peculiarities in his character, 32—obtains permission to print Gray's poems, 32—presents Gray with a copy of the folio Homer, 34—Beattie's letter to him relative to a proposed edition of Virgil, 35, 36—his obstinacy in continuing the Academy, 36—his career on the decline, 36—his brother's death, 37—determines to discontinue the Academy, 38—goes to London with his pictures, 38—exhibits them, 39—his letter to Lord Mountstuart, 88—they are sold to great disadvantage, 39—is consoled by Dr Hunter, 40—leaves London, reaches Edinburgh, and dies, 40—his character by Professor Richardson, 41, 42—his Catalogue of Pictures, 43—notice of him in the Literary Society, 44, 45—one of his daughters married to Arch. Maclauchlane, 84—his last letter to his partners, 136, 137.

Foulis, R. & A., their edition of Shakespear, 21, 23—Milton, 34—projected Virgil, 36—receive premiums from the Select Society, 30, 31—their insolvency, 45—their affairs settled, 46—paper used by them, 138.

France, 11, 17.
Freer, Dr Robert, 134.

Georgia, 14.
Germany, 85.
Gibb, Dr Gavin, 134.
Glassford, Campbell, and Ingram, 136.
Glassford, John, of Dougaldston, 18, 38.
Glasgow, 1, 2, 4, 5, 6, 9, 10, 11, 12, 13, 14, 15, 18, 20, 27, 28, 30, 31, 33, 34, 43, 82, 83, 84, 86, 87, 89, 90, 121, 128, 129.
———— Courant, 6.
———— Journal, 6, 7, 8, 128.
———— University of, 4, 11, 13, 40, 88, 119, 120, 122, 126, 127, 128, 129, 130, 132.
Glencairn, Earl of, 87.

Glencairn, Countess of, 87.
Govane, Donald, younger, 5, 120, 121.
Graham, Alexander, 132.
———— Archibald, 134.
———— John, of Dougaldston, 133.
———— Dr Patrick, 134.
Gray, the poet, 32, 33, 34.
Guido, 24, 43.

Hamilton, Balfour, and Neill, 31, 32.
———— Duke of, 85, 88.
———— Earl of, 85.
———— Gavine, 86.
———— Gilbert, 134.
———— John, 120.
———— Dr Robert, 9, 132.
———— Thomas, 133.
———— Professor William, 134.
———— William, of Bangour, 23, 28, 29.
———— town of, 6.
Harvie, Thomas, 4, 5.
Harvock, 19, 20.
Harwood, Dr Edward, 14.
Heinsius, Daniel, 35.
———— Nicholas, 35.
Hemsterhuse, 22.
Holland, 3, 18, 22, 82.
Holmes, David, 121.
Hope, Dr, 134.
Horace [immaculate edition], errors in, 14.
Hume, David, 132, 133.
Hunter, Dr William, 40.
Hutcheson, Dr Francis, 10, 11, 15, 16, 20, 21.

Jackson, Mr, 134.
Jameson, George, 81, 82.
———— William, 122.
Jardine, Professor, 133.
Jeffray, Dr James, 134.
Ingram, Archibald, 18, 38.
Inverary, 6.
Inverness, 6.

Johnstone, James, 9.
Johnstone, John, 120, 121.
Irvine, Dr, 133.
Irvine, town of, 6,

Kennedy, Thomas, 88.
Kilmarnock, Earl of, 128, 129.
Kilmarnock, town of, 6.

Lanark, 6.
Law, John, 125.
Le Clerc, 90.
Leechman, Dr William, 15, 132.
Lindsay, Hercules, 132.
Lithgo, Gideon, 2.
Lockhart, Dr John, 134.
London, 7, 20, 21, 26, 28, 33, 34, 38, 39, 40, 43, 44, 129, 136.
Loudon, John, 120, 126.

M'Diarmid, Rev. Hugh, 134.
M'Donald, Rev. Andrew, 134.
Macgill, Dr Stevenson, 134.
Mackay, Rev. Mr, 133.
Maclauchlane, Archibald, 84, 88.
M'Leod, Dr, 134.
Macturk, Professor, 134.
M'Ure's History of Glasgow, 5.
Mar, Earl of, 7.
Marshall, Dr, 134.
Maxwell, George, 132.
——— Sir John, of Netherpollok, 120.
——— of Polloc, family of, 3.
Meikleham, Dr, 134.
Melville, Thomas, 132.
Millar, Professor James, 134.
——— Professor John, 15, 133.
——— John, Advocate, 134.
——— Dr Richard, 134.
Mitchell, James, 88.
Montrose, family of, 37.
Moor, Elizabeth, 43.

Moor, James, 43, 127.
——— Dr James, 12, 16, 21, 22, 23, 127, 128, 129, 130, 131, 132, 133.
Morthland, Charles, 4, 120, 121, 124.
Mountstuart, Lord, 88, 89.
Muirhead, George, 129, 133.
——————— Lockhart, 134.
Mure, Elizabeth, 127.
——— William, of Caldwell, 132.
Mylne, Professor, 134.

Naples, 86.
Newall, Miss Peggy, 9.
Northumberland, Countess of, 19, 20.
——————————— Earl of, 19, 20, 21.

Ogilvie, Mr, 133.
Orr, John, of Barrowfield, 13.
Oswald, George, 133.
Oxford, University of, 11.

Paris, 17, 136.
Paton, George, 43.
Patterson, Marion, 9.
Paul, Robert, 87.
Pinkerton, John, 29, 81, 82.
Pitt, Mr, 27.
Pollok, Maxwells of, 3.
Pope, 21, 29.
Primrose, Lady Dorothy, 87.

Raeburn, Sir Henry, 40.
Ramsay, Allen, 10.
——— the Chevalier, 12.
Rankin, Rev. Dr, 134.
Raphael, 36, 40, 43, 85, 86, 87, 88, 89.
Reekie, John, 23.
Reid, Dr Thomas, 16, 133.
Richardson, Professor, 15, 16, 29, 31, 32, 39, 41, 130, 132, 133.
Ridpath, George, 4.
Robert II., 127.

Robison, Professor, 133.
Rome, 86.
Roscommon, Earl of, his poems, 20.
Ross, Andrew, 120, 121.
Rosse, George, 12, 14, 132.
Ruat, William, 132.
Rubens, 81, 85, 88.

Salier, L'Abbé, 22.
Sanders, Robert, of Auldhouse, 2, 3.
Sandford, Mr, 88.
Scotland, 3, 17, 18, 40, 81, 82, 83, 85.
Scougal, 82.
Selkirk, Earl of, 27, 128, 129, 136.
Shakespear, 21, 23.
Shawfield, Campbell of, 25, 88.
Simson, Professor John, 120, 121.
——— Dr Robert, 13, 120, 121, 131, 132.
Smellie, Alexander, 31.
Smith, Dr Adam, 16, 25, 28, 132.
Spalding, John, 82.
Spotiswood, James, 46, 129.
Stalker, Andrew, 7, 8, 9, 127.
St Andrews, 6.
St Clare, Dr Robert, 122.
St Johnstoun, 6.
Stephens, Robert, 12, 20.
——— Henry, 31.
Stevenson, Dr Alexander, 133.
Stirling, Principal, 4, 120, 121, 122.
Stirling, town of, 6.
Strange, Robert, 29.
Stranraer, 6.
Stuart, Dr Gilbert, 130.
——— Walter, 132.
Sunderland, Earl of, 85.

Tassie, James, 90.
Tasso, 90.
Tay, Firth of, 7.
Taylor, Dr, 133.
——— Principal, 134.
Titian, 85.
Townshend, Right Hon. Charles, 19.
Trail, Dr., 131.
——— Professor, 35, 133.

Urie, Robert, 5, 8, 9.

Vandyke, 81, 86.
Vatican, 21, 22, 89.

Wait, Mr, 133.
Walker, Dr, 133.
Warburton, Dr, 131.
Watson, James, 3.
Wedderburn, Mr, 28.
Whitefield, Rev. George, 14.
Wight, Dr, 133.
Williamson, Dr, 133.
Wilson, Dr Alexander, 13, 133.
Wilson & Baine, 12.
Wilson, Patrick, 134.
Wodrow, Dr, 37.
——— Robert, the historian, 4.
Wright, Rev. John, 133.

Yair, bookseller, 24.
Yorke, Mr, 86.
Young, John, 130, 133.
——— Thomas, 121.
——— Dr Walter, 134.

APPENDIX TO NEW EDITION.

BOOKS PRINTED BY THE FOULISES NOT INCLUDED IN THE PREVIOUS LIST.

[*The collection of Foulis' books in the Mitchell Library includes the following works not in the foregoing list. The books after 1776 were of course issued by the nephew and other successors.*]

1741.
Ramsay (Chev.), A Plan of Education, third edition, 12mo.

1744.
Marcus Antoninus. Imperatoris eorum quae ad seipsum Libri XII., 12mo.
Abridgment of Mr. Locke's Essay concerning Human Understanding, sixth edition, 12mo.

1748.
Cicero. De Inventione Rhetorica, 18mo.

1750.
Webb (B.), Dissertatio Philosophica Inauguralis de Imperii Civilis Origine et Causis, sm. 4to.

1751.
Scougal (Henry), Discourses on Important Subjects, 18mo.
Addison (J.), The Drummer; or, The Haunted-House. A Comedy, 18mo.
Prior (M.), Poems on Several Occasions, 2 vols., 12mo.

1752.
Milton (John), Poems on Several Occasions, 18mo [Foulis? no imprint].
Dryden (J.), The Spanish Fryar; or, The Double Discovery, 12mo.

1754.
Fenelon, Dialogues of the Dead, 2 vols., 12mo.

1755.
Ramsay (Chev.), Travels of Cyrus, 2 vols., 24mo.

1756.
Cicero. In Catilinam Orationes iv., 12mo.
Hutcheson (F.), De Naturali Hominum Socialitate, 12mo.

1758.
Addison (J.), Rosamond. An Opera, 12mo.

1759.
Prior (M.), Poems on Several Occasions, 2 vols., 12mo.
Addison (J.), A Discourse on Ancient and Modern Learning, fourth edition, 12mo.

1763.
Barr (Jas.), An Easy Introduction to Latin Grammar, 12mo.

1764.

Craig (Wm.), The Character and Obligations of a Minister of the Gospel, 12mo.

1765.

Confession of Faith, etc., 8vo.

1767.

Xenophon. Institutio Cyri, 4 vols., 12mo.

1768.

M'Gill (Wm.), The Prayer of Our Saviour, etc., 12mo.

1769.

Boswell (J.), Corsica : A Poetical Address, second edition, 12mo.
Death of Artho, and the Death of Fraoch, two Ancient Poems, 8vo.
Glover (R.), Leonidas. A Poem, 18mo.

1771.

Prior (Matt)., Poems on Several Occasions, 2 vols., 18mo.
Steele (Sir Richard), The Conscious Lovers. A Comedy, 12mo.

1772.

Homer. Odyssey. Translated by A. Pope. 3 vols., 18mo.
Milton (J.), Paradise Regain'd, 2 vols., 18mo.

1774.

Butler (S.), Hudibras, 2 vols., 18mo.
Mason (W.), Poems, 2 vols., 18mo.

1775.

Dryden (J.), Original Poems, 2 vols., 18mo.
Addison (J.), Poems on Several Occasions, 18mo.
Lyttleton (Lord), Poems, 18mo.
Collins (W.), Poetical Works, to which are added Mr. Hammond's Elegies, 18mo.
Shenstone (W.), Select Works, third edition, 18mo.
Aikenside (Dr.), The Pleasures of Imagination, 18mo.

1776.

Young (E.), The Complaint : or, Night-Thoughts, 2 vols, 18mo.

1777.

Cornelius Nepos. Imperatorum Vitae, third edition, 12mo.
Sallust. Opera, 12mo.
Sophocles. Œdipus Tyrannus, 12mo.
Moor (J.), Elementa Linguae Graecae, 12mo.
Collins (W.), Poetical Works, to which are added Mr. Hammond's Elegies, 18mo.
Œschylus. Choephorae, small 4to.
Anacreon. Carmina, 12mo.

1778.

Isocrates. Panegyrica, 12mo.
Homer. Ilias, 2 vols., 12mo.
Virgil. Bucolica, Georgica, et Æneis, 2 vols., folio.

1779.

Æschines. In Ctesiphontem Oratio, 12mo.
Drummond (W.)., Polemo-Middinia, small 4to.

1780.

Moor (J.), Elementa Linguae Graecae, 12mo.
Synopsis Metaphysicae, seventh edition, 12mo.

1781.

Richardson (Wm.), Poems, Chiefly Rural, fourth edition, 12mo.

1783.

Anacreon. Carmina, 12mo.
Anacreon. Odai, 12mo.
Eutropius. Historiae Romanae, 18mo.
Phaedrus. Fabulae, 12mo.

1784.

Virgil. Bucolica, Georgica et Æneis, 12mo.
Thomson (J.), Poetical Works, 2 vols., folio.
Euripides. Medea, 12mo.
Cicero. De Officiis ad Marcum Filium, 12mo.

1785.

Theophrastus. Characteres Ethici, 12mo.
Lucan. Pharsalia, 12mo.
Pope (Alex.), Poetical Works, 3 vols., folio.

1786.

Parnell (T.), Poetical Works, folio.
Riddell (J.), Malvina, a Tragedy, 12mo.

1787.

Gray (T.) and Collins (W.), Poetical Works, folio.
Lyttelton and Hammond, Poetical Works, folio.

1788.

Pindar. Olympia, 12mo.

1789.

Plato. Apologia Socratis, 12mo.

1791.

Bibliotheca Universitatis Glasguensis Catalogus, folio.

1792.

Anacreon. Carmina, etc., 12mo.

1793.

Moor (J.), Elementa Linguae Graecae, 12mo.

1796.

Æschylus, Tragoediae, 2 vols., 8vo.

1806.

Euripides. Tragoediae Selectae, 2 vols., 8vo.

A SHORT HISTORY OF THE ART OF PRINTING IN GLASGOW FROM ITS INTRODUCTION IN 1638 TILL 1740.

[*From Macvean's Notes to M'Ure's "History of Glasgow."*]

THE art of printing was first introduced into Scotland in 1507, and it appears to have been carried on for a few years and then relinquished; at least we can find no works which had been printed between the years 1510 and 1536. A few works are still preserved which were printed between 1536 and 1560.

After the reformation the art was encouraged and carried on successfully in Edinburgh; and occasionally at Stirling and St. Andrews. In 1621 the magistrates of Aberdeen appointed Edward Raban printer to the city, with a salary and a small sum (paid quarterly) from each boy at the grammar school.

In 1638, George Anderson was induced to commence printing in Glasgow; and it is said that the magistrates allowed him a salary: a dancing master and a fencing master received similar encouragement. Anderson had previously printed several works in Edinburgh, in king James' college, in the years 1637—8. As very few of the works printed by Anderson in Glasgow are now to be found, we give a list of all that we have been able to discover. It is probable that he printed many of the pamphlets relating to the troubles before the commencement of the civil war; but as they generally appeared without the name of place or printer, we shall only give those which we have observed with his name. The first work which we have found, and probably one of the very first printed in Glasgow, is:

The protestation of the Generall Assemblie of the church of Scotland, and of the noblemen, barons, gentlemen, borrowes, ministers and commons; subscribers of the covenant, lately renewed, made in the high kirk, and at the mercate crosse of Glasgow, the 28, and 29, of November, 1638. *Printed at Glasgow by George Anderson in the yeare of grace* 1638
Boyd's four letters of comforts for the deaths of the earl of Haddingtoun, and the Lord Boyd; with two epitaphs, 8vo, ... 1640
Boyd's battle of Newburne, &c., *the second edition*, 8vo, ... 1643
Boyd's Crosses, Comforts, and Councels, 8vo, ... 1643
Row's Hebrew Grammar, 12mo, ... 1644
Boyd's Garden of Zion, 2 vols. 8vo, ... 1644
Boyd's Holy Songs of the Old and New Testament, 8vo, ... 1645
Dickson on the Epistles, 4to, ... 1645
Boyd's Psalms in English meeter, *the third edition*, 12mo, . . . 1646
Dickson, on Matthew, *Printed in Hutchison's Hospital*, 4to, . . . 1647
Boyd's Psalms (Roxb. Cat.) 12mo, ... 1648

George Anderson appears to have died in 1648, and we find "The heirs of George Anderson" printing in Edinburgh from 1649 to 1652. For about ten years after the death of Anderson there does not appear to have been any printer in Glasgow. In 1655 principal Baillie had one of his pamphlets printed in London. Andrew Anderson, the son of George, printed in Edinburgh in the years 1654—5. In 1658 we find him printing in Glasgow, where he continued till about 1661, when he returned to Edinburgh. He printed the following works at Glasgow:

Silvester Rattray Auditus novus ad Sympathia et Antipathia, 8vo,	1658
An ceud chaogad do Shalmaibh Dhaibdh (the first fifty psalms of David translated by the synod of Argyle), 12mo,	1659
Foirceadul Aithghearr Cheasnuighe (the Shorter Catechism in Gaelic by the Synod of Argyle), *the second edition*, 12mo,	1659
Binning's Common Principles of the Christian Religion, 12mo,	1659
Confessio Fidei, 12mo,	1660

Andrew Anderson was succeeded by Robert Sanders, who was the only printer in the west of Scotland for many years. He styled himself printer to the city of Glasgow, and frequently used a cut of the city arms in his title pages, with the motto "*Lord, let Glasgow flourish through the preaching of thy word.*" Watson informs us that he died about 1696. He printed a great many books, tracts, poems, and other small pieces, which it would be impossible to collect or enumerate; we shall only give a list of a few of the works from his press in chronological order:

God's sovereignty his sacred majestie's supremacie, &c., in a sermon before the parliament, 31 March, 1661, by Mr. Hugh Blair, minister at Glasgow, 4to,	1661
Young's Breviary of the latter persecutions, 12mo,	1663
The civil warres of Great Britain and Ireland, 4to,	1664
The Life of Bruce by Barbour, 12mo,	1665
Rattray Silvester, Prognosis Medica, 8vo,	1666
The Cherrie and Slae,	1668
A Godly Sermon of Peter's Repentance, 12mo,	1669
The Dreadful Character of a Drunkard, by Andrew Jones, 12mo,	1669
The New Testament, *black letter*, 12mo,	about 1671
Welch's anatomy of Popery, 8vo,	1672
Sir D. Lindsay's works, 12mo,	1672
The blessedness of the dead that die in the Lord, a sermon at the funeral of the late Marques of Montrose, the 23 of April, 1669, 4to,	1673
The certainty of death and judgment, a sermon at the obsequies of the Marchioness of Montrose, Jan. 23, 1673, by Arth. Ross, 4to,	1673
Theses Philosophicæ, 4to,	1674
Baxter's full and easy satisfaction which is the safe religion, 8vo,	1674
Ferguson on Thessalonians, 8vo,	1675
Durham on the Ten Commands, 4to,	1676
The whole duty of man, 12mo,	1678
Sir David Lindsay's works, 12mo,	1683
Ross's Sermon before the commissioners at Glasgow, 4to,	1684
Dialogorum Sacrorum, 12mo,	1685
William Saunders, Elementa Geometricæ, 8vo,	1686
Gray's Spiritual Warfare, 12mo,	1688
The Votes and Proceedings of Parliament vindicated, 4to,	1689
Wallace, *black letter*, 12mo,	1690

Theses Philosophicæ, 4to, ... 1693
Lilius (Gul.) Monita Pedagogica, 8vo, ... 1693
Guthery's Great Interest, 12mo, ... 1695
A modest apology in answer to the bishop of Derry, 12mo, ... 1696

 Sanders was succeeded by his son, who was styled Robert Sanders of Auldhouse; he carried on the business till about 1727; he was also a bookseller, and kept a shop above the Grammar School Wynd, and afterwards in the Saltmarket; a few of the works printed by him are added.

Jameson's Fundamentals of Hierarchy examined, 4to, ... 1697
The conflict in conscience of a dear Christian woman Bessie Clarkson, 12mo, . 1698
Calendarium Lunæ Perpetuum, &c. (By John Law). 4to, ... 1699
The new Wife of Beath, *in verse*, 12mo, ... 1700
Dickson's True Christian Love, 12mo, ... 1700
Guild's Harmony of all the prophets, 12mo, ... 1701
The conflict in conscience of Bessie Clarkson, 12mo, ... 1703
A Lecture preached in the church of Paslay by Mr. John Bard, 12mo, . 1703
The Christian's Pocket Book, or a bundle of familiar exhortations, 12mo, . 1703
An account of the last words of Christian Kerr, 12mo, ... 1703
The Testament of the Twelve Patriarchs, *wood cuts*, 12mo, ... 1704
Theses Philosophicæ, 4to, ... 1708
The Psalms of David, *very small size*, ... 1711
The last heavenly speech of Viscount Kenmuir, 12mo, ... 1712
Sir David Lindsay's works, 12mo, ... 1712
Gesta Romanorum (in English), 12mo, ... 1713
A Sample of Jet Black Prelatic Calumny, 4to, ... 1713
Craghead's Advice to Communicants, 12mo, ... 1714
Ferguson's 932 Scottish Proverbs, 12mo, ... 1716
Adam Bell Clim of the Clough and William of Cloudeslie, 12mo, . . 1716
Mead's Almost Christian, 12mo, ... 1717
Binning's Common Principles of the Christian religion, 12mo, . . 1718
Robin Redbreast and the Wren, or Robin's complaint on the vanity of the times, com-
 pyl'd above 60 years ago 12mo, ... 1719
Bunyan's Holy War, 12mo, ... 1720
Wedderburn's David's Testament opened, 12mo, ... 1721
Durham on the Song of Solomon, 12mo, ... 1723
Gray's Works, 12mo, ... 1724
Binning's Heart Humiliation, 12mo, ... 1725
Nasmith's Entail of the Covenant of Grace, 12mo, ... 1725
A Godly Dream by Lady Culross, 12mo, ... 1727

 Hugh Brown printed here from 1712 to 1720. In 1714 he published *the Jacobite Curse*, and assumed the title of Printer to the University. The principal and professors published the following advertisement: "At the college of Glasgow, Decr. 6, 1714. The faculty being informed that a pamphlet called the Jacobite curse, lately published, bears to be printed by Hew Brown, printer to the university of Glasgow, albeit the said Hew Brown never was printer to the university but only imploy'd by Donald Govan, who some months past was allowed to print, within the college, and with whom the faculty is yet under communing about his being constituted printer to the university; they thought fit to call the said Donald before them, and having interrogated him if he knew any thing of the printing of that pamphlet, he declared the same was printed without his knowledge, and when he was abroad. The faculty considering the premises do order an advertisement to be put in the public prints, shewing that the said Hew Brown never was printer to the university, and that he printed the pamphlet without the knowledge of Mr. Govan; tho' he was only employed by him & not by the university." His name appears at the following works :

A Sermon preached at the opening of the Synod in the church of Air by John Anderson minister in Dumbarton, 4to,	1712
The Tarif settled by the French king in 1664, 4to,	1713
The Last Words of Mr. Donald Cargill on the Scaffold, 12mo,	1713
The Jacobite Curse, or Excommunication of King George, 4to,	1714
Anderson's defence of Presbyterian Church Government, 4to,	1714
Anderson's letter to Stewart of Pardovan, 4to,	1717
Tennoch's Examination of the Overtures con. kirk sessions,	1720

James Hart printed in the university, we have only seen this single work printed by him,—

An Account of a Conference betwixt Mr. John Steel minister at Old Cumnock, and John Adamson a disorderly preacher, 4to,	1714

Donald Govan printed in the college, the only work with his name which we have seen is

The Merchant's Companion, by W. Newall, 8vo,	1715

James and William Duncan printed "in the foot of the Saltmarket" in 1718. It has been asserted by some of our historians that Dr. Wilson was the first who introduced the art of making types into Scotland. This is not however the case. Watson in his account of the Scottish printers says, "In 1711 Mr. Peter Rae, a presbyterian minister, set up a small house at Kirkbride, near Dumfries, which he continues going. He is an ingenious man, having made a press for his own use, and is making some advances (1713) toward the founding of Letters. In 1718 we find "James Duncan letter founder in Glasgow." The types used by Duncan are evidently of his own making, they are rudely cut and badly proportioned; and in some of his founts the letter e is one third smaller than the other letters. He deserves credit however for the attempt, and his founts are not much inferior to those used by the other Scottish printers at that time. James and William Duncan printed

Snuff, a Poem, by James Arbuckle, 8vo. Glasgow, printed in the year	1717

This has no printer's name, but it appears to have been by Duncan.

Rulers Sins the causes of National Judgments; a Sermon preached at the Fast Decr. 26, 1650, by Mr. Patrick Gillespie minister at Glasgow, 4to,	1718
Jameson Spicilegia Antiquitatum Ægypti, 8vo,	1720
Anderson's Six Letters upon the Overtures concerning Kirk Sessions, 12mo,	1720

After 1720 they printed separately; James continued till about 1750. In the title page of M'Ure's history he stiles himself printer to the city: a few of the works printed by him are added.

Brevis Introductio ad Grammaticam Hebraicam et Chaldaicam in usum Academicorum
Glasguensium, 12mo, ... 1721
The fulfilling of the Scriptures, 8vo, ... 1721
The Last Testimony of John Neisbit, never before printed, 12mo, . . . 1722
The Confession of Faith, 12mo, ... 1727
Stevenson's Rare Cordial, 12mo, ... 1729
The Father's Catechism, in a legacy to his eighth children, by W. L., 12mo, . 1729
The Confession of Faith, 12mo, ... 1732
M'Ure's View of the City of Glasgow, 8vo, ... 1736
The Pleasant Art of Money Catching, by Mr Alex. Montgomery, 12mo, . . . 1740
William Duncan printed from 1721 till 1760 ; he printed
Glotta, a Poem by Mr Arbuckle student in the university of Glasgow, 8vo, . . 1721
The Negative discussed by Mr William Wright, 12mo, ... 1721
The History of all the Kings of Scotland from Fergus I. to the end of Q. Ann's reign ;
with the lives of several famous persons, 8vo, ... 1722
A new edition of the Life and Heroick Actions of the renoun'd Sir William Wallace, (by
William Hamilton) 8vo, ... 1722
Buchanan's History of the Surname of Buchanan, &c., 4to, ... 1723
Vincent's Catechism, 12mo, ... 1728
Brook's Mute Christian, 12mo, ... 1736
A Cry from the Dead ; or, the Ghost of the famous Mr James Guthrie appearing, &c.,
8vo, ... 1738
Thomas Crawfurd printed, Naphthali, or the Wrestlings of the Church of Scotland, 8vo, 1721
Mr Alexander Carmichael & Company printed in Glasgow college in 1730.
Carmichael's Believers Mortification of Sin by the Spirit, 12mo, ... 1730
A Letter to the Rev. Professor Campbell, 8vo, ... 1731
Vincent's True Touchstone, 12mo, ... 1732
Brook's Mute Christian, 12mo, ... 1734
Alex. Carmichael and Alex. Millar printed several works in company.
The Life and Acts of the most famous and valiant Champion Sir William Wallace, 12mo, 1736
The Acts and Life of the most victorious Conqueror Robert Bruce King of Scotland, 12mo, 1737
The New Testament, 12mo, ... 1737
Alexander Millar printed, The Cruel Watchman ; a Sermon by Mr. Samuel Rutherford,
12mo, ... 1738
Decerpta ex Ovidii Metamorph. with Clarke's translation, 8vo, ... 1739
The whole Prophecies of Scotland, England, France, Ireland, and Denmark, prophesied
by Thomas Rymer, &c., 8vo, ... 1739
Love's Heaven's Glory ; and Hell's Terrors. *Glasgow college by Alexander Miller*, 12mo, 1741
John Robertson and Mrs. M'Lean printed Craighead's Advice to Communicants, 22mo, 1740

Robert Urie and company printed in the Gallowgate in 1740. Urie has the merit of being the first printer to improve the art which had been gradually degenerating from the time of George Anderson. He printed several works for Robert Foulis, who was a bookseller for two years before he commenced printing ; the Terence of 1742, was printed by Urie for R. Foulis. Urie printed the Glasgow Journal, which was commenced by Andrew Stalker in July 1741. There had been a paper previously printed here called the Glasgow Courant, and the West

Country Intelligence. No. 1 appeared Nov. 11, 1715, and No. 67, which appears to have been the last, in May 1716.

Urie continued to print a great variety of books till his death which happened in 1771.

In 1741 Fobert Foulis was a bookseller in Glasgow, and in 1741—2 we find several works "printed *for* Robert Foulis." In 1742 he set up as a printer, and after a few years was joined by his brother Andrew. They carried out the art to a higher degree of perfection than it had hitherto reached in Scotland. Their editions of the classics are well known and highly esteemed. Our limits do not permit us to give an account of the numerous books printed by them, of which we have a list of about 300 different works. We are happy however to learn that a gentleman is collecting materials for a history of these eminent printers, which is also to include a list of the works printed by them. Andrew Foulis died in 1775, and his brother Robert in 1776.

A CHRONOLOGICAL LIST OF GLASGOW PRINTERS UP TO 1800.

[*From Mason's "Public and Private Libraries of Glasgow," page 148.*]

MATERIALS are not as yet available for a complete List of these predecessors of our present typographers, but the following names are among them. The dates following the names are not intended to show either the beginning or the ending of the work of each respectively, but merely the date of the first book of each now in the Mitchel Llibrary. A few of the names are those of publishers, not printers:—

Anderson (George),	1638	Urie (R. & Co.),		1741
Anderson (Andrew),	1658	Paton (George),		1741
Sanders (Robert),	1664	Foulis (R. & A.),		1742
Hepburn (Andrew),	1689	Duncan (David),		1743
Sanders (Robert) 2nd,	1697	Smith & Hutcheson,		1745
M'Lean (Archibald),	1706	Hall (John),		1748
Brown (Hugh),	1713	M'Callum (John),		1749
Govan (Donald),	1715	Orr (John),		1750
Duncan (J. & W.),	1720	Bryce & Paterson,		1752
Crawford (Thomas),	1721	Knox (James),		1752
Duncan (William),	1726	Newlands (J.),		1753
Glasgow College (no name),	1730	Duncan (Wm., junr.),		1753
Carmichael (Alex.),	1731	Marshall (W.),		1755
Stalker (Andrew),	1732	Henderson (A. & J.),		1757
Carmichael & Millar,	1736	Bryce (John),		1760
Millar (Alex.),	1738	Smith (Robert),		1762
Robertson (John),	1739	Mair (Patrick),		1764
Robertson & M'Lean,	1739	Walker (William),		1767

Galbraith (Joseph),	.	.	1768	Niven (David),	. . .	1785
Hutcheson (Charles),	.	.	1768	Duncan (James),	. . .	1788
Duncan & Co.,	.	.	1770	Miller (Ebenezer),	. . .	1790
Tait (Andrew),	. .	.	1770	Reid (John),	. . .	1791
Duncan (R. & T.),	.	.	1771	Turner (James),	. . .	1791
Reid (Daniel),	. .	.	1772	Macaulay (Andrew),	. .	1792
Smith (William),	.	.	1772	Miller (Wm.),	. . .	1792
Adam (Alex.),	. .	.	1773	Paton (W.),	. . .	1795
Chapman (Robert),	.	.	1775	Gillies (James),	. . .	1796
Robertson (J. & J.),	.	.	1777	Duncan (J. & A.),	. . .	1796
Chapman & Duncan,	.	.	1779	Mundell (James),	. . .	1797
Bell (William),	. .	.	1781	Napier & Khull,	. . .	1798
Robertson (J. & M.),	.	.	1783	Cameron (A.),	. . .	1798

The pre-eminent name, whether for the excellence, the accuracy, or the quantity of the work, is that of Robert & Andrew Foulis. The reputation of the brothers is more than local, more than Scottish, more even than British; for their books are mentioned with respect by bibliographers the world over. Together with Baskerville of Birmingham, they most worthily upheld for many years the character and excellence of the provincial press. To whatever excellence of execution their successors in the art may have attained, the older work still holds its own in correctness of composition, in evenness of inking, in accuracy of register, and, in short, in all the qualities which render a well-made book a delight to its possessor and an object of envy to his friends.

THE END.

ALEX. GARDNER, PRINTER, PAISLEY.